Different

CROWN
BUSINESS
NEW YORK

Different

Escaping the
Competitive Herd

Youngme Moon

Illustrations by Lynn Carruthers

STANDING OUT IN A WORLD WHERE CONFORMITY REIGNS BUT EXCEPTIONS RULE

Copyright © 2010 by Youngme Moon

Published in the United States by Crown Business,
an imprint of the Crown Publishing Group,
a division of Random House, Inc., New York.
www.crownpublishing.com

CROWN BUSINESS is a trademark and CROWN and the Rising
Sun colophon are registered trademarks of Random House, Inc.

Grateful acknowledgment is made to The Coca-Cola Company for
permission to reprint lyrics from "I'd Like to Buy the World a Coke."

Crown Business books are available at special discounts for bulk
purchases for sales promotions or corporate use. Special editions,
including personalized covers, excerpts of existing books, or
books with corporate logos, can be created in large quantities for
special needs. For more information, contact Premium Sales at
(212) 572-2232 or e-mail specialmarkets@randomhouse.com.

Originally published in hardcover in the United States by Crown
Business, an imprint of the Crown Publishing Group, a division
of Random House, Inc., New York, in 2010.

Library of Congress Cataloging-in-Publication Data

Moon, Youngme.
    Different / Youngme Moon.
      p.   cm.
    Includes bibliographical references and index.
    1. Marketing.   2. Competition.   I. Title.
    HF5415.M58   2010
    658.8—dc22   2009032752

ISBN 978-0-307-46086-8
eISBN 978-0-307-46087-5

Printed in the United States of America

Book design by Lauren Dong
Illustrations by Lynn Carruthers
Cover design by Jamie Keenan
Cover photograph: Getty Images

20   19   18   17   16   15   14   13   12

First Paperback Edition

For Robert, Jalen, and Tailo

contents

contents

introduction

when my eldest son was in second grade, he started bringing home poems to memorize. Each week, a new poem. So each night, we would memorize a verse, repeating the words over and over again until they were securely mimeographed into the folds of his supple little brain.

At first, I did this without question or complaint. But as the days passed, I found myself reconsidering the purpose of these mental calisthenics. You see, for the past ten years I have been an educator myself, a professor of marketing at the Harvard Business School, where every semester my colleagues and I require our students to master a very particular language. We expose them to the "grammar" of business—essentially a set of frameworks and best practices—and we make them rehearse this grammar over and over again, in case study after case study.

But what I have learned from this experience is that while a commitment to rehearsal will almost always produce competence, it will almost always produce a kind of automaticity, too. There is a reason why so many educators rail against rote learning, and it is that they know it can have the self-defeating effect of promoting a kind of mindlessness. Once we over-learn something, we cease to know it anymore at all. This is what I see happening in the world of business today. In industry after industry, business professionals have become so practiced in a particular way of doing things that they appear to have forgotten the point of it all—which is to create meaningful and compelling product offerings for people like you and me. This is not to say that these folks lack the requisite business skills; rather, it is to say that they have become almost *too* proficient, in the same way that a well-oiled production system can be scarily proficient at churning out one perfectly identical clone after another.

I may be a business academic, but I am also a citizen, a wife, and a mother, and my guess is that I probably experience the world in much the same way that you experience it. Which means that when I leave my house to purchase something as prosaic as a bottle of shampoo or a carton of juice or a pair of sneakers, what happens to me is probably very similar to what happens to you: I am confronted with a dizzying array of options from which to choose. In every aisle, in every store, what used to be, just a generation ago, a relatively modest selection of, say, four or five, has somehow turned into an indistinguishable selection of eleventy thousand. Meanwhile, there is a redundancy in the way these products are advertised to me as well. To be fluent in the language of product marketing is apparently to have polished the language of hyperbole, and so I am assured, again and again, that each one of these products is NEW AND IMPROVED. Everything is BIG BETTER BEST.

And yet here is the thing. We have all lived through quite a lot in the past few years. This most recent recession, in particular, hit us all pretty hard, and although each one of us had little choice but to weather through in our own private way, I can't help but believe that the storm refocused us all in some collective way, too. I remember right after the first wave of the recession hit—the housing market had just imploded and the credit markets had frozen up—feeling almost grateful that I didn't live in one of the more sumptuous estates in our town, one of those homes that I used to so admire. I also remember reading stories in the newspaper about how people, even those who were financially secure, had begun rethinking their most basic consumption patterns. It was as if our notions of aspiration and acquisition had shifted, overnight. Excess was out, replaced by a more thoughtful consideration of the stuff with which we filled our homes, our closets, our lives. *The age of abundance is over,* I remember thinking, *not because things are no longer abundant, but because abundance has lost its status as our reigning aspiration.*

I have always believed that there is a part of business that is an art, and if I had to describe the particular complexion of this art, I would describe it as the art of calibration. In my mind, this is where the marketer must step in: The marketer needs to be able to ascertain the dimensions of our desire—paying heed to the things that we want, yes, but paying equal heed to the things that we do not. It may be true that our desire has no limit, but it certainly has a shape. Yet what is missing from business today is a sensitivity to the contours of our aspiration. As a culture, we have moved well past the point where we are impressed by the traditional markers of affluence—the profusion of look-alike choices, the embarrassing display of whistles and bells. Nevertheless, to this day . . . one need only to walk into a store to experience the degree to which business doesn't seem to get this.

A decade ago, product marketing could afford to be as over-the-top as rock and roll. Hyperbole came with the territory; a lack of originality was no big deal. To get the crowd's attention, all you needed was to memorize a couple of predictable chord progressions, nail a catchy chorus, and then hit the stage with confidence, energy, and enthusiasm. The trick was to be loud, excessive, bold. A few smoke and mirrors didn't hurt, either. Today, that kind of marketing is likely to appear as vacuous as a 1980s heavy metal band. Today, the business maestros more likely to garner a listening audience are the ones who understand that, in this era of more thoughtful consumption, louder is seldom better, and more-of-the-same almost never adds up to the best.

I wrote this book because I believe that what most of us are looking for today is a sound more resonant. A sound more meaningful. A vibration that we are able to experience, in our bones, as being somehow . . . *different*. And so that is what this book is about: It is an exploration of what it means for a business to commit to giving us this. It is an exploration of what it means for a business to decide to *be* different.

I do this by venturing into the world of sameness, in search of difference. I seek to identify the outliers, the anomalies, the iconoclasts—the players who have rejected well-rehearsed business routines in favor of an approach more adventurous. These are the players with a feel for improvisation, for experimentation, the players who have somehow managed to build brands and create products that are striking a genuine chord with even the most jaded among us.

Along the way, I make the argument that it is time for business professionals—marketers, in particular—to begin letting go of some of the things that they have come to regard as best practice. This is no easy challenge; as I tell my students: Learning is easy; forgetting is hard. Yet this is precisely what I believe is necessary if business is to build a new culture of consumer engagement, one that creates, at the very least, the possibility that we will begin listening again.

Incidentally, this past year, it was my younger son's turn to start second grade. As expected, it wasn't long before he—like his brother before him—began bringing home poems to memorize. Each week, a new poem. And so each night, I found myself dutifully feeding him his lines, over and over again, my déjà vu complete.

Only this time, my heart wasn't in it. Because over the years, I have come to believe that a poem perfectly memorized is a poem too easily recited. And a poem performed without effort is a poem that has lost all meaning.

—

I have a friend, a businesswoman, who claims that she can absorb the gist of a business book, any business book, in under an hour. Of course, whether or not you're impressed by her claim depends on whether you've ever read one yourself. Most business books are written for easy digestion. They are reductive in the way that subway maps are reductive; the elimination of unnecessary information creates a kind of conceptual isolation that is functionally efficient to the extreme.

But reduction can come at a cost. A few years ago, Edward Tufte, who resides at Yale and spends most of his time thinking about the presentation of information, published a monograph (*The Cognitive Style of PowerPoint*) about the cognitive hegemony of the world's most popular presentation software. As Tufte pointed out, the unfortunate price of simplification is, well, over-simplification. Not to mention the additional tax paid out in the form of pedantry. Imagine if you were to go to a dinner party only to discover that all of the guests had decided to present their stories in PowerPoint format. Yes, the evening would be informative, but it would also be a bore.

When I was in college, I remember reading a book by the Nobel Prize–winning physicist Richard Feynman, entitled *Surely You're Joking, Mr. Feynman!* What was interesting about the book was that it appeared to be nothing more than a compilation of rambling anecdotes—about his personal life, his teaching, his work. And yet the weight of these anecdotes crept up on you, so that by the time you finished the book it was impossible to regard it as anything less than a finely honed indictment of the scientific discipline.

What Feynman seemed to understand was that there are in fact two ways for a scholar to contribute to our understanding of something. The first is to adopt the PowerPoint approach, which is to take a complex phenomenon and attempt to distill it down to its core. The second is to do the reverse: to take a complex phenomenon and attempt to shed new light on it, not by removing information but by layering on unexpected shades of nuance, from unexpected sources. This is what Feynman did: He wove his subject into the broader tapestry of everyday life. He added richness, texture, context. He was a man I wish I could have invited to dinner.

There are other examples of this, of scholars who have written books that have influenced my own approach to writing. The physician Atul Gawande has produced two books (*Complications* and *Better*) about medicine and the health care system in this country. Gawande's books are a complicated brew—they touch on the professional and the personal, they are alternately dispassionate and impassioned, and together they transformed the way I thought about medicine. John Stilgoe has written a book entitled *Outside Lies*

Magic; it transformed the way I thought about modern architecture. When I was a graduate student, Don Norman's seminal *The Design of Everyday Things* transformed the way I thought about technology and function.

All of these works exist across wildly different disciplines, and yet they have something very much in common: They were written by scholars who were able to bring their respective disciplines to life, by humanizing them somehow, without dumbing them down. Their relationship to their work is akin to the one Calvin Trillin has to food, which is to say that they regard their subject—whether it be medicine, or architecture, or technology—as constituting one small piece of a much larger fabric. These are writers who meander, certainly, but only as a means of getting straight to their point. Meanwhile, they manage to be the opposite of pedantic, which is another way of saying that they are comfortable with the knowledge that things can be true and false at the same time.

Their books inspire, because although they provide a running commentary of all that is wrong with their respective disciplines, they do not stop there. I have always thought that the way to keep criticism from devolving into cynicism is to make it the starting point rather than the punctuation mark, and that's what these writers do: They look hard to identify the good amid the bad, and when they find it, they shine a light on it, they celebrate it, they encourage us to learn from it. If scholarship is a conversation, then in my mind these are the ones who make the most compelling conversationalists—the ones braving the unfamiliar dialect, the ones pushing the dialogue forward in unexpected and provocative ways.

—⁓—

I wrote this book because I believe that marketing has become the soundtrack of our generation. It is setting the pulse, it is creating the rhythm—not just for what we consume, but for what we crave, what we love and what we hate. Against this backdrop, there are some insights that are not well represented by linear thinking. And so this is a book full of contradictions. Juxtapositions. Sideways connections.

In addition, every year, I tell my students that marketing is the only function within the organization that is expressly designed to sit at the intersection where business meets people. *Real* people. And the problem with real people is that they don't see the world the same way a businessperson does. They don't speak the language of bullet points; they don't organize the world into flowcharts and frameworks. People, real people, view the world more organically. They are idiosyncratic. They are unpredictable. They are beautifully disorganized.

This book could be described in much the same way. It is intimate. It is organic. It is idiosyncratic. It's even a bit disorganized. But in my mind, that's okay, because my aspiration is not to be deductive; it is to be discursive in the unpredictable way that people are discursive. In business, just as in life, sometimes the most illuminating insights can emerge from the throwaways.

I should add that the nicest note I've ever received

from a student was one that said: "The difference between your course and every other one taught at the Harvard Business School is that it was so human. It was a class about *us*, disguised as lessons in business."

That's what this book is. It's a book about *us*, disguised as lessons in business.

a preview

imagine that you are standing in the middle of the cereal section of your local supermarket. Your job is to select a cereal you've never tried before, ideally one you'll end up enjoying. How would you go about doing it?

If you happen to be someone who has eaten cereal on a fairly regular basis throughout your life, the task is actually not that hard. In all likelihood, you'd simply walk down the aisle, mentally eliminating entire batches of cereals at once—say, all of the children's cereals . . . or anything that looked too sugary. You'd then winnow your selections further by applying a secondary set of filters—for example, anything with granola . . . or anything high fiber. After you'd narrowed the aisle down to a small subset of cereals—maybe six or seven brands—you'd layer on a few additional criteria—perhaps dismissing anything containing raisins or anything in an ugly box—until, boom, you'd made your selection.

The whole exercise would probably be over in a matter of minutes, unless of course you happen to be the type of person who is really persnickety about your breakfast fare, in which case it might take a bit longer. Regardless, what would be impressive about your performance, irrespective of the outcome, would be the intelligence of your approach. Somehow, you have learned to deconstruct the product category the way a product marketer would: as a cascading set of subcategories and mini-subcategories. Somehow, you have learned to segment the product array across a range of dimensions, and somehow, you have learned to make distinctions between brands that come down to the most minute of details. In other words, you may not have realized it, but somewhere along the way, you became a category expert, a cereal connoisseur.

Now imagine a martian standing in the same aisle, faced with the same task. What was easy for you would be completely daunting for him. Even assuming his superior intelligence, parsing the variation among products would take hour upon hour. For this poor creature, all of those cereal boxes would look bewilderingly the same.

Why? Because where a connoisseur sees the differences, a novice sees the similarities. Where a connoisseur can discern subtle shades of distinction based on nuanced asymmetries, a novice lacks the necessary filters to canvas, to organize, to sift an assortment in a meaningful way. Where a connoisseur can navigate a category with effortless intuition, a novice will struggle to find beginning, middle, or end. Shopping in this regard can be beyond experiential; it can be phenomenological.

You could repeat this same exercise again and again, across product after product, with similar results. Try explaining to a foreigner the difference between Crest and Colgate. Try explaining to a child the difference between a Honda and a Toyota. When I visit a Foot Locker with my husband, he will cruise the store like an oenophile seeking a rare varietal. I, on the other hand, am a category outsider. So while he roams, I will park myself in a corner of the store and feel overcome by the sameness.

—⁓—

There is perhaps no better way to get a glimpse into the mass consumption values of a culture than to visit the place where the inhabitants of that culture purchase the stuff of daily living—soap, food, shoes. If aliens were to visit a grocery store or a drugstore in this country, they would have to conclude that we are a people hooked on the pleasures of picking needles out of haystacks—of selecting a cereal among an ocean of cereal boxes, of selecting a bar of soap among an ocean of soap bars. And in many ways, they would be right. We take for granted how frequently we thrust ourselves into the position of having to make purchase decisions in the face of overflowing product profusion.

This is particularly true in mature product categories. When a product category is nascent, it tends to be dominated by a much smaller set of products, or even a single product. The original PowerBar. The original Walkman. Coke and Pepsi. As the category evolves, however, the number of product alternatives within the category tends to grow exponentially. Today, PowerBar alone produces more than forty different varieties of its energy bar, and the energy bar category has grown to include more than sixty assorted brands. Today, Sony produces more than two dozen variations of its Walkman, and the personal stereo category consists of more than a hundred options. In fact, one quick way to gauge the maturity of a category is to simply track the number of product variants in it.

EVOLUTION of a PRODUCT CATEGORY

And yet it would be a mistake to assume that product proliferation begets product diversity. On the contrary, as the number of products within a category multiplies, the differences between them start to become increasingly trivial, almost to the point of preposterousness. Try it. Pick a random product category such as soap, or cereal, or shoes, and make a list of what is different among the products within the category. The list will probably be long, but an overwhelming number of these differences will almost certainly be trifling. Put another way, the category has reached the point where it is possible for product heterogeneity to be experienced as product homogeneity. Which is not to say that the distinctions between products are not real; it is simply to say that they are real only in the same way that synonyms have discrete connotations. Blue is dissimilar to red in a different way than teal is dissimilar to navy.

For a business, this is when competing in the category can become problematic. Because this is when it can require a category expert—a connoisseur—to negotiate the category with any kind of ease.

——

In many ways, product connoisseurship can be compared to language. It belongs to that special breed of knowledge that can be portal to a new world of understanding and interpretation. It is access; it is membership; it is authority. And if the non-fluent appear clueless by comparison, it is because they are. Lacking the means to penetrate the world with any kind of intelligence, non-speakers are outsiders in the most literal sense.

One of the easiest ways to acquire connoisseurship is through immersion. If every day were declared to be Halloween, it wouldn't be long before we would all be authorities on candy.

Easier still is to be introduced to a product category when it is at a relatively young age. The reason for this is that product categories tend to unfold in a cumulative fashion: a cell phone that used to be good only for phone calls is upgraded and developed over time to send text messages, take photos, capture video, and so on. If you are able to internalize these product complexities as they develop, your command of the category can deepen without much willful effort. You simply evolve and mature as a consumer as the market itself evolves and matures.

It is far more mentally demanding to have to catch up to a category midstream. If you were to decide one day to become a chef, for example, your education would have to include not only learning how to cook but learning how to make fine distinctions between this type of cooking utensil and that type of cooking utensil, between this type of pepper and that type of pepper. And although parts of the process might feel pleasant enough, parts of it would probably feel much like homework, and it would take both time and effort before you could make informed choices with a comfort level approaching that of a category veteran.

Given this, category connoisseurs are not difficult to identify. The giveaway is almost always in the modus operandi. I have a co-worker who is fastidious about the writing utensils she purchases; she will think nothing of spending up to half an hour in the pen-and-ink section of Staples, studying the assortment like an epicure in search of the perfect meal. She has made herself a connoisseur of the category. I have a neighbor, a road warrior, who is exacting about the kind of laptop he uses; he will scrupulously compare weight differentials and battery life among the dozens of portables on the market. He has made himself a connoisseur of the category.

In categories in which we are cognoscenti, we are in many ways ideal customers. We are buying machines. We are discriminating, we are informed, and we have internalized the logic of the category with all of its various permutations. We are able to appreciate the peculiarities of a Canon EOS 40D versus a Nikon D90, or 2x Ultra Tide versus Ultra Purex Powder, and can thus maneuver our way around the category, not just with confidence but with erudition. And because connoisseurship often goes hand-in-hand with devotion, we typically have strong affinity for the category. We are aficionados in addition to being experts.

―――

But expertise, too, can have a life cycle. At some point, the differences between products can become too incremental for even category devotees to appreciate anymore. A lover of language may delight in synonyms, but it's hard for anyone to see the point in a hundred different ways to say the word "blue."

We can all think of categories in which this has happened to us. Like my neighbor, I used to invest time looking for the perfect laptop offering the ideal balance of price, weight, and processing power, but the category has gotten away from me now . . . so these days, any laptop in the lightweight subcategory is fine by me. Similarly, I used to insist on buying a particular size, type, and brand of detergent . . . but I've long since stopped trying to keep up with the latest developments in the detergent aisle.

In other words, there can come a point in the maturation of category when even the most frequent buyers stop believing the comparative diligence is worth the effort: The homemaker who is willing to give a cheaper brand a try. The road warrior who no longer cares about owning the hottest new portable. This can be a dangerous inflection point in the life cycle of a category: when the proportion of comparative differentiators to non-differentiators starts to shift direction. Now, the category is composed of a shrinking number of devotees who are focused on differences that seem almost idiosyncratic, along with a growing number of customers who are beginning to suspect that the differences simply don't matter anymore.

When a category reaches this point, I would contend that it is possible to start segmenting the market according to nothing more than the coping strategies customers have begun to adopt to deal with the growing market cacophony. I'll introduce this segmentation scheme to you later on in the book; suffice it to say that the customer segments include pragmatics, reluctants, opportunists, and so on. What all of these segments have in common is that they are made up of folks whose affection for the category has dissipated over time, replaced by some combination of indifference, confusion, and cynicism.

―――

Why is this dangerous? Because at the heart of business success is the ability to compete; the ability to compete, in turn, is dependent on the ability to differentiate from competitors. Differentiate or die, or so the saying goes. And yet when a category reaches a point where there are a growing number of consumers skeptical about the differences between products and brands, the differentiation within the category is at risk of being rendered meaningless.

One indication that a category has reached this point is that devotion to it not only declines but begins to look downright silly in its manifestation. To be on top of the category requires an obsessiveness about the most inconspicuous differences. We have all met folks like this—people who are a little too fussy about the kind of socks they wear or who are unnaturally strident about the merits of one brand of fabric softener versus another. Loyalty in this context requires the same kind of shamelessness as extreme price sensitivity: You have to be willing to reveal that you care deeply about something that the typical person would consider petty. This is a bad scenario for a business— when devotion demands a measure of fastidiousness, a level of engagement that borders on the eccentric.

When a category has reached the point when it's possible to make fun of the people who still believe in the differences across products, it has reached the point of what I refer to as heterogeneous homogeneity: The differences are there, but they are lost in a sea of sameness. Note that the mockery quotient of a category is directly correlated to the amount of meaningless differentiation in it.

—⁓—

There are truisms in business, just as there are truisms in sport, in play, and in life—self-evident, obvious truths that require little or no persuasion. Buy low, sell high. Know thy competition. Listen to your customers. These are the axioms that have not only achieved the status of conventional wisdom in the world of commerce, they have become part of our modern business reflex. And because these wisdoms have become congenital almost, when they are called into question, we tend to be not just defensive, but dismissive.

When basketball installed the twenty-four-second rule, it did so to maximize the game's high-scoring potential; from then on, it went without saying that in order to win it was necessary to score, and score a lot. This is what made the ascendance of the 1956–57 Boston Celtics such a discontinuous moment in the history of the sport: The Celtics were a team of stoppers, not scorers. Led by their magnificent defensive virtuoso, Bill Russell, they defied conventional wisdom by winning the championship not just once, but eleven times in thirteen years.

At the time, most fans were apt to dismiss Russell as an aberration, an athletic wonder with an uncanny ability to do what others could not. More generally, when a challenger comes along and successfully flouts the existing orthodoxy, the initial reaction is usually to treat the exception as exceptional, rather than to treat the rule as potentially faulty. Fair enough. Sometimes an aberration is exactly that—an aberration.

Sometimes, however, the aberration can be a harbinger of something else, a shift in the landscape, perhaps, that carries with it the potential to undermine the foundations upon which we reflexively operate. In the

NBA today, defense wins championships, and everyone knows it. Why have we come to believe this? Because once the exceptions start to occur with enough regularity, conventional wisdom begins to transform under the weight of new evidence until, finally, the old truth is revealed as a myth—a false collective belief or, in some cases, an ideological relic.

What makes things tricky is that sometimes the difference between a truth and a myth is nothing more than time. A generation ago, offense *did* win championships; today, the opposite is true. In the 1960s and '70s, the words "new and improved" really *meant* something to people; today, those same words don't mean much at all. What is true in the light of day can become false in the dark of night. This is the problem with shifts: They tend to happen in real time, which means that there are going to be moments of ambiguity when remnants of the old truth still hold together, even as remnants of it are falling apart.

I believe that we're seeing one of those shifts in business today. One of the theses of this book is that in category after category, it has become apparent that competitive differentiation is a myth. Or to put it more precisely, in category after category, companies have gotten so collectively locked into a particular cadence of competition that they appear to have lost sight of their mandate—which is to create meaningful grooves of separation from one another. Consequently, the harder they compete, the less differentiated they become.

In these categories, there is a proliferation of sameness rather than differentiation, at least in the eyes of all but the most ardent category connoisseurs. Products are no longer competing against each other; they are collapsing into each other in the minds of anyone who consumes them. The fact that Verizon and AT&T Wireless are locked in fierce competition is meaningless to anyone who can't discern any significant difference between their offerings. If martians were to land in this country, they would think there was a conspiracy of brands colluding in almost every category.

The extent to which true competitive differentiation has become a rarity becomes most evident when you simply take a look around you. In so many consumer categories—whether it be cereal, cell phone plans, or sneakers—it is difficult to name a single brand that stands out for its uniqueness.

I am reminded of a game my children like to play called perpetual tag. It's something of a mysterious game, involving an odd combination of running, chasing, tagging, freezing, and rock-paper-scissors. From what I can tell, the essential ingredients of the game are as follows: Any combination of kids—regardless of age, gender, or running ability—can play against each other; there is enough randomness built into the outcome to make it easy for weaklings to stay in the game yet difficult for jocks to dominate; at any given time, someone is winning, but never by very much and never for very long (the lead changes hands with too much frequency); and there is no natural end to the game—it can theoretically go on forever. In short, the beauty of the game, at least from a parenting standpoint, is that while lots of energy gets expended and everyone gets winded in the process, the circadian rhythm of the game makes it almost impossible for anyone to stand out.

The metaphor should be obvious. The central premise in part 1 of this book is that in so many consumer categories, differentiation has become hard to come by because we have fallen into a pulse of competition that in and of itself has become an impediment to its emergence. In part 1, I also contend that businesses that find themselves locked into this particular pattern of competitive engagement have become masters at producing product categories filled with heterogeneous homogeneity, or dissimilar clones if you will. Which is to say that they have become masters of a particular form of imitation. Not differentiation, but imitation. Yet because this particular form of imitation is cloaked in the vernacular of differentiation, the myth of competitive separation lives on in the minds of the managers running these firms. Meanwhile, the emperor has no clothes and most consumers know it.

—⁓—

Fortunately, there is a second part to the narrative.

When sceneries change and deeply ingrained truths start coming apart at the seams, the first to let go of the myth has the advantage. In part 2 of this book, I contend that if one were to identify the most compelling business stories of the past two decades, a disproportionate number of these stories, in category after category, could best be described as exceptions to the rule. They could be considered the business version of the 1950s Celtics, which means that their ascendance should be viewed as a harbinger that the landscape is shifting and that old wisdoms are on the verge of surrendering to the new.

What this means is that a careful examination of these outliers can yield telling insights. It's easy to forget that this has always been true. Anyone can learn how to write or paint or play music, but the virtuosos who have historically merited our most thorough exegesis have been those who were willing to stretch the boundaries of text, of music, of art, in new directions. In field after field, past experience has taught us that the ones to pay attention to are the ones who understand the rules so well that they also understand the urgency to break them. These are the players who force us to confront the frailty of our assumptions.

I believe that the same can be said of the world of business. As a percentage, the number of companies who are truly able to achieve competitive separation in their respective categories—to break through the noisy clutter, to create genuine emotional resonance with consumers—is depressingly small, and yet these outliers have much to teach us about the limitations of some of our most deeply held business assumptions. So while part 1 of this book may read like a critique, part 2 will read very much like a celebration, of these iconoclasts and their ways of doing business.

Of course, there are pitfalls in writing a book in which the mavericks are the champions. There is fashion in academia, just as there is fashion in clothing, media, and entertainment, and the idea of the rule breaker as protagonist has become Harry Potter—trendy to the point of cliché. That's why the objective in part 2 of the book isn't so much to coronate these mavericks as to deconstruct and demystify what they've accomplished in a manner that makes their achievements accessible to the rest of us.

———

At the same time, I should be perfectly clear: This book is not a how-to. The reason I find how-tos discomfiting is that there is always the slim chance that people may actually take them on faith. What business-people need today is a fresh set of insights, not a fresh set of instructions. Thus, in part 3 of the book, I set out, in a series of reflections, to begin a conversation about a new way of thinking about competition generally, and competitive differentiation specifically.

In this regard, the challenge in writing this type of business book is that all of the good sentences have already been written. Break all the rules. Ignore conventional wisdom. Be radical. Discard the old; embrace the new. So the question is, how does one give weight to words that probably already feel over-used?

There is no easy answer to this. However, if you were to visit the travel section of your local bookstore, you would find two types of travel books. Dominating the section would be a set of books of the travel guide variety: Fodor's *Caribbean 2010. Italy for Dummies.* Frommer's *Europe from $85 a Day.* These are instruction manuals really, filled with explicit travel advice on where to go and what to do, delivered in the form of listings, bullet points, rankings, and so on.

But tucked alongside this vast selection of instruction manuals would also be a second set of books offering an alternative form of discourse on the same topic: Bill Bryson's *Notes from a Small Island.* John McPhee's *Coming into the Country.* Paul Theroux's *To the Ends of the Earth.* Here, you would likely find nothing more than some author's personal ruminations and observations of, say, a recent visit to the English countryside, or an arduous trek through the Himalayas, or a meandering walk in the woods. Meanwhile, there would be very little explicit travel advice, for the unspoken reason that anything so pedantic would only detract from what might potentially be this type of book's most lingering effect—which is to serve as a gentle reminder that wherever you go, what matters less is what you are looking at, but how you have committed to see.

I mention this because a key argument in this final section of the book is that process drives outcomes; i.e., that the way people engage in the practice of competition tends to cultivate conformity and convergence in business. This is why I believe we need a new praxis. We need to develop new habits, new disciplines, and new conventions around the exercise of competition. Most important, we need to build a new culture of competitive engagement that creates, at the very least, the possibility that an extraordinary outcome may emerge.

So allow me, if you will, to take you on a walk through the world of consumption as I see it. I may meander a bit, and even slip into academic mumbo jumbo every once in a while, but keep in mind that the value of a diary like this one is intended to be measured on the rebound. Which is my way of saying that, at the end of the day, what matters less is what's on the page, but what's in your head as you read it.

part 1

the competitive
herd

(critique)

the herd

instinct

when I was a young girl, I had a teacher who used to encourage her students to drink glass after glass of milk. Somehow, she had developed the notion that milk boosted one's intellect. For this teacher—a scholar by heart and by training—there was nothing more precious, no currency more valuable, than intelligence.

On occasion, one of us would ask her point-blank, "What's intelligence?" Each time, she would offer a different response:

"Intelligence is a baby's first words."

"Intelligence is the joke Hyun-Ju made in math lesson this morning."

"Intelligence is three brothers holding hands."

"Intelligence is yellow."

Her responses would drive us crazy, and now, some thirty years later, it's interesting to consider why. As children, we were in effect asking her to describe something for us in the most straightforward way we knew how. And although she would always respond in a manner that was open and even forthcoming, her actual responses would build on expressions that bore no apparent relation to what she was describing. The whole thing was pretty maddening, to be honest with you.

That said, today I'm inclined to be more sympathetic with my elementary school teacher. Over the years, I've learned that description can be a delicate challenge for the describer, too; the deeper you try to dig into the essence of the thing, the further you have to reach to come up with the right words to do justice to what you're describing. The nice thing is that it's possible to mix-and-match words in an infinite variety of combinations to help you do this; what's tough is that when they're mixed-and-matched in an unexpected or overly ambitious way, the rendition can become almost uninterpretable to the person on the other end.

As an adult, I've been on both sides of this. When I hear a critic describe a particular wine as "somewhat challenging, but with significant cerebral appeal," or having "a touch of menthol and green eucalyptus on the entry," along with "generous notes of acacia honey and vanilla on the finish," I'm never quite sure what I'm supposed to do with the information. Likewise, there are few things I find as frustrating as poring over a two-thousand-word review of the latest movie release only to walk away still feeling unsatisfied. It's as if the reviewer got so caught up in the joys of prose that he neglected to address the reader's most fundamental questions. Yes, the acting was "industrious" and the lighting "nervy," but was the movie any good? Was it worth seeing?

On the other hand, each year, about two hundred

students enroll in my class. If you were to ask me to characterize this group of students to you, you'd probably expect me to do so along predictable lines. You wouldn't expect me to tell you that they are soundproof, or squeezably soft, or that they need daily watering. You'd expect me to tell you that they are smart, witty, kind, or outgoing. A good description is one that captures distinctiveness along dimensions that make sense to us. If it doesn't do this, we have no means of figuring out where to place the described entity in our heads.

But even though I know this, I'd still be tempted to liven up my description of my students to do them better justice, which would eventually lead me back to the thorny issue of vocabulary. When it comes to portraying something as complex as, say, an individual or a group of individuals, there remain too many words to play with. A person could be described as obnoxious, quaint, acerbic, fragile, loquacious, or energetic. It's the endless variety problem again.

This is where a uniform method of description can be useful. What a uniform method of description does is put discipline around the words. It creates a common ground for our characterizations by enforcing a shared set of touch points, at the same time heading off an endless game of vocabulary mix-and-match.

Consider, for example, one of the more popular methods of description around: the standard personality test. A personality test is a measurement tool designed to depict an individual's persona along a predetermined set of dimensions. There are obviously many variations of the test, but a rudimentary one can be devised from just two (fairly self-explanatory) dimensions: dominance/submissiveness and friendliness/unfriendliness.

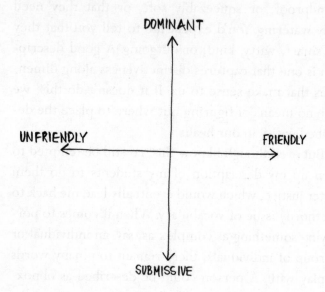

What's appealing about this kind of measurement tool is the extent to which it can capture a disproportionate amount of information with parsimony. Most personality tests involve four or five dimensions, but even a crude two-dimensional metric can be curiously revealing. To say that someone is an "unfriendly-submissive" is to say a tremendous amount about them. Sure, you could extrapolate an additional set of descriptors (e.g., "passive aggressive," "sulky," "resentful") to flesh out the complexion more fully, but the nucleus of the description is there. This is what a good descriptive metric does—it gets to the heart of the matter; it captures the core of a characterization that could otherwise go on forever.

In addition, it's impossible to study a 2 × 2 map such as this one and not project yourself onto it. It wouldn't take much to figure out which quadrant you belonged in; similarly, it wouldn't take much to figure out where to place your friends, your family members, your co-workers.

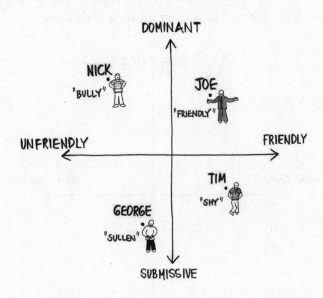

This is the second element of a good descriptive metric—it invites comparison. It depicts individual distinctiveness in a way that makes it possible to see connections that were not obvious up to that point. (It can be oddly addictive in this regard.) It generates that "oh, this is why George has always reminded me of Richard" pang of association.

What businesspeople do with products and brands is not unlike what psychologists do with individuals: They rely on descriptive tools to lay bare the essence of what they're trying to understand. The metrics themselves are also generated in an analogous fashion: by asking people to provide their perceptions of a product or brand, and then using those perceptions to plot the product or brand on a diagram such as this one:

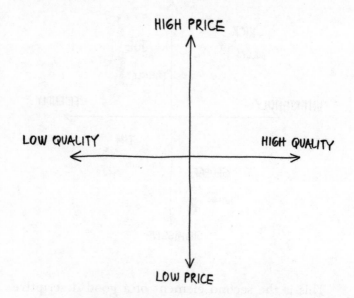

Brand managers call these diagrams positioning maps, and they spawn different versions depending on the product category. A typical positioning map for the hotel category, for example, might be anchored by the dimensions of price, luxury, service, and location. A positioning map for the laptop category might be anchored by the dimensions of price, features, quality, and weight.

Once created, this positioning map can end up being the linchpin for a company's competitive strategy, not only because it provides a snapshot of the brand's personality in the eyes of consumers but also because it does so relative to the competition. By plotting all the category offerings on a single map, companies can compare and contrast their own strengths and weaknesses to those of other players.

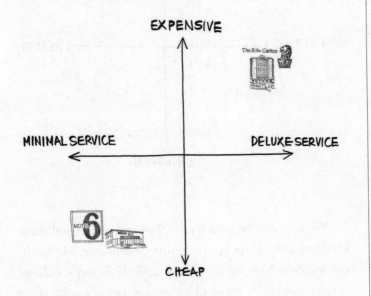

For consumers, a snapshot like this can be informative for a symmetrical reason. To resurrect that poor alien from the previous chapter, think of how helpful a basic 2 × 2 would have been in navigating that byzantine cereal aisle:

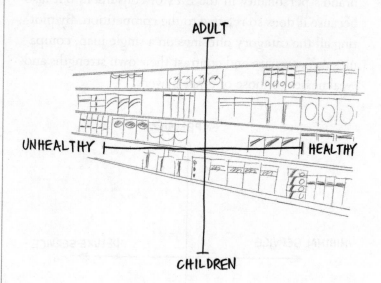

We may not be aware of it, but we've all used these kinds of snapshots at one point or another. My earliest introduction to *U.S. News & World Report*'s college report probably took place some twenty-odd years ago. At the time, there were two things I found startling about the report. The first was how radical it was in its transparency. In an era in which universities had become comfortable relying on amorphous perceptions of "reputation" to attract students, the report held nothing back. It exposed the empirical guts of these institutions—tuition costs, SAT scores, instructor-student ratios—with a granularity that would have been otherwise impossible for the average applicant to obtain. It was like seeing "inside" a college for the first time.

The second was the extent to which the report invited comparison. In effect, the report was a competitive positioning map rendered in tabular form, and the consolidation of the data made it impossible not to hold one school up against another, across this dimension or that dimension.

Again, as consumers, we seek out these kinds of comparative metrics all the time. The data may not necessarily be available to us in graphical form, but no matter. Whether it be data involving universities, hotels, or automobiles, the metrics can be oddly addictive—empowering, even—in their ability to dispatch so much information with so much efficiency.

—————

But measurement can cut both ways. In track and field, we happen to measure speed, and so we cultivate a nation of speedsters. If we happened to measure running style, we would cultivate a nation of gazelles. The minute we choose to measure something, we are essentially choosing to aspire to it. A metric, in other words, creates a pointer in a particular direction. And once the pointer is created, it is only a matter of time before competitors herd in the direction of that pointer.

In the 1980s and 1990s, a number of prominent

hospitals agreed to make public their mortality rates. The agreement was considered a breakthrough in hospital openness, promising to give patients the kind of insider view into hospital quality that they'd never been privy to before. If a hospital's mission is to heal, then what better way to audit the performance of a hospital than to track the ultimate measure of that healing ability?

What soon became evident, however, was that a hospital's mortality rate is a function of an elaborate host of factors—including the type of patients it admits, the amount of experimental research its doctors conduct, and the degree of care it provides—each of which can heavily conflate the intended meaning of the metric.

To put it more bluntly, it soon became evident that the easiest way for a hospital to improve its mortality rate would be to stop admitting the sickest patients. Yet if all hospitals were to do this, the overall effect on the medical system would be chilling: There would be fewer hospitals accepting the most challenging cases, experimenting with the riskiest treatments, becoming specialists in the most intractable disease areas. Hospitals wouldn't get better, they would simply become more like each other.

In recent years, the college ranking system has come under fire for precisely this reason—for dampening the likelihood that universities will experiment with models of pedagogy that may not reflect well in the metrics. The rankings have made it hazardous to be a nonconformist.

This, then, is the problem with uniform systems of measurement: The more entrenched a system of measurement, the more difficult it is for a deviant, an outlier, or even an experimenter to emerge. Another way to say this is to say that a competitive metric, *any* competitive metric, tends to bring out the herd in us. The dynamic can be likened to the observer effect in physics, only applied with too little foresight: The act of measurement changes the behavior of the thing being measured.

—

Here is another example. Jeep is a brand with a legitimate heritage in the sport utility category, and in my mind, anyway, deserves much of the credit for the development of an SUV market in this country. Twenty years ago, its brand was synonymous with the concept of rugged four-wheel-drive transportation, such that a perceptual metric comparing Jeep's image along this dimension against, say, the image of competitors like Nissan or Toyota, would have heavily favored Jeep. On the other hand, a comparison of these same brands along a dimension such as, say, reliability, would have favored Nissan or Toyota:

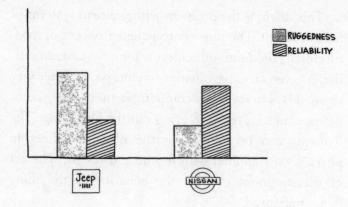

Today, both of these diagrams would look more like this:

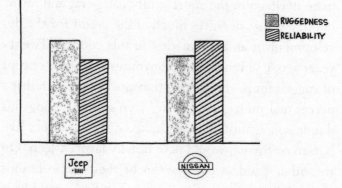

What has happened in the interim? Quite simply, ruggedness and reliability have become standard metrics against which car companies measure themselves in the SUV category, which means that brands lagging along these dimensions have raced to catch up. Multiply this effect across all of the other dimensions that SUVs have come to be measured against—gas mileage, safety ratings, comfort, and so on—and the cumulative effect has been a gradual homogenization of the offerings within the category over time:

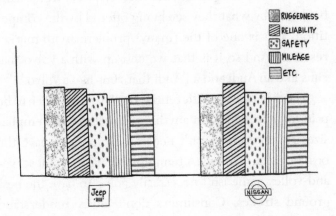

This same competitive trend can be seen in category after category. Ten years ago, Volvo was a brand known for its practicality and safety, whereas Audi was a brand known for its sportiness; nowadays, Audi outperforms Volvo in safety tests, whereas Volvo's advertisements work to assure customers that its cars are fun to drive.

The dynamic is not unlike a popularity contest in which everyone tries to win by being equal parts friendly, happy, active, and fun. Or an election campaign in which all the candidates try to be charming, serious, humble, and strong. Once everyone starts doing it, no one stands out.

Even consumers are not immune to this behavior. Ask Volvo drivers for suggestions on how to improve the brand and they will tell you that they love its safety focus, but could you please improve its sex appeal; ask Audi drivers the same question and they will tell you the converse. Indeed, the problem with asking consumers what they want is that not only will they ask for things they're not getting, but their requests will usually be driven by what they see being offered by the competition. This is one of the (many) problems with market research. And so it is that we end up with a Volvo that runs like an Audi and an Audi that runs like a Volvo.

There is a cost to differentiation. There is a price to be paid for excellence, in anything. A college that emphasizes great teaching isn't necessarily going to have the best research facilities. A tennis player with a great serve-and-volley game isn't necessarily going to have the best ground strokes. Consumers don't always understand this. This is why, if you're looking for a compromise solution, then yes—take a poll, conduct some research, survey the people. But if you're looking for a *unique* solution, the last thing you should do is ask for a vote.

~~~

When I first started teaching as a graduate student many years ago, I came up with what I thought was a benign way to motivate the dozen or so students enrolled in the small seminar I was leading. At the midway point of the semester, I decided to provide them with some fairly detailed feedback on their performance to date. A few days later, one of my strongest students walked into my office bearing a troubled look. I had given him a mid-semester evaluation that looked something like this, relative to his peers:

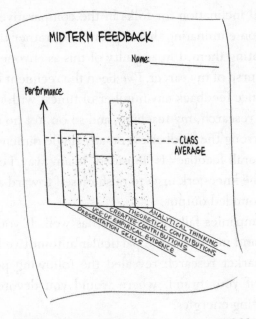

The question he had for me was, what could he do to improve his creative contributions to our discussions?

It was only after he had left my office and a few additional weeks of the semester had passed that the cumulative effect of my feedback became apparent to me: Just about everyone in my class was focused on improving their weaknesses. The most creative thinkers in the room were intent on improving their analytical skills, while the most analytical thinkers in the room were intent on improving their creative contributions. This was evident both in their written assignments and in their discussion comments. No one was playing to their strengths anymore. As a result, our class discussions had begun to lose their sparkle.

A funny thing happens the minute you begin to capture comparative differences on paper: There is a natural inclination for folks in the comparative set to focus on eliminating those differences, rather than accentuating them. I'm as guilty of this as anyone. Over the course of my career, I've been the recipient of performance feedback any number of times, with respect to my research, my teaching, and so on. Yet no matter how strong the feedback is on any single dimension, if the overall feedback is "lopsided" in any way, I experience the knee-jerk urge to push myself toward a more well-rounded output.

Companies fall into this trap as well. If you were the brand manager for a particular automotive brand, and market research revealed the following perceptions of your brand, where would you devote your marketing energies?

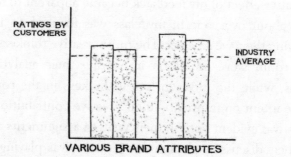

MARKET RESEARCH

HOW CUSTOMERS PERCEIVE YOUR BRAND

RATINGS BY CUSTOMERS

INDUSTRY AVERAGE

VARIOUS BRAND ATTRIBUTES

My guess is that you'd feel pressure to address the "vulnerabilities" in your brand. Meanwhile, it might not even occur to you to do the opposite—to double down on your strengths, further extending the distance between you and your competitors.

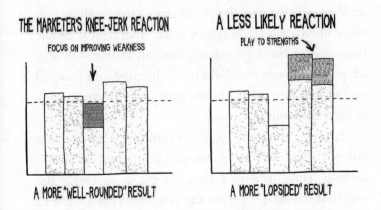

THE MARKETER'S KNEE-JERK REACTION

FOCUS ON IMPROVING WEAKNESS

A MORE "WELL-ROUNDED" RESULT

A LESS LIKELY REACTION

PLAY TO STRENGTHS

A MORE "LOPSIDED" RESULT

And yet ultimately, this is how well-meaning efforts to monitor your competitive position—whether it's through brand positioning maps, market research, or any other form of competitive analysis—can turn into a cattle prod for homogenization. Back when I used to give that mid-semester feedback to my students, it was never my intention to diminish the overall quality of our class discussions by stifling the differences among them, but this is in fact what I did. Similarly, when organizations deliver performance feedback to their employees, the intention is not to cultivate a homogeneous workforce, but this is in fact what can occur as a result.

The truth of the matter is, true differentiation—*sustainable* differentiation—is rarely a function of well-roundedness; it is typically a function of lopsidedness. The same can be said for excellence. If you were to meet a brain surgeon who also claimed to be a pediatric orthopedist who also claimed to be a specialist in Botox treatments, you'd likely view all of his credentials with skepticism. Why? Because intuitively you understand that excellence on any extreme almost always involves a trade-off. It's like the typical movie portrayal of the high school football coach who also happens to teach social studies—he may be a football genius, but he's probably not going to win any awards in the classroom.

Applying the same logic, if Hummer were to come out with an advertising campaign boasting a family-friendly ride, it would hurt its claim to being the toughest motherf*cker on the road. If Ferrari were to come out with an advertising campaign that underscored its commitment to child safety, it would hurt its claim to being the baddest sports car on the market. Negative trade-offs are not only a marker of excellence, they are a marker of differentiation. This is as true for products and brands as it is for brain surgeons.

For businesses, however, the impulse to move to a more well-rounded output can be hard to resist. And the cumulative effect of this, in too many cases, is a herdlike regression toward the mean. As I write this, Starbucks is experimenting with offering breakfast value meals in its coffee shops while McDonald's is experimenting with putting coffee bars in its fast-food outlets.

———

In animal behavior, the defining characteristic of a herd is the absence of conspiracy; it is the uncoordinated behaviors of self-seeking individuals that create the deception of a single, unified group moving as one. When you see a herd in action, what you are seeing is coordination without a coordinator, or what scientists would refer to as a self-organizing system. Elsewhere, I use the phrase "organic collusion" to evoke precisely this kind of unpremeditated collaboration.

A hive is a self-organizing system. An ant colony is a self-organizing system. Flocks, traffic flows, the stock market—all of these are self-organizing systems.

The easiest way to understand how self-organizing systems operate is to essentially break one down. In the 1980s, Craig Reynolds became intrigued by the phenomenon of birds flying in coordinated flocks. A computer animator by training, he decided to try to build a program that would generate a facsimile of flocking behavior on the screen. He began by programming each artificial bird to abide by three simple rules: (1) avoid crowding or colliding into nearby birds; (2) keep up with nearby birds (by flying at roughly the same heading and speed); and (3) drift in the direction of the average position of nearby birds.

Although he knew he had more work to do before he was finished, he went ahead and tested the simulation using just these three rules. To his surprise, without any further programming, the birds flocked perfectly. Reynolds's contribution to the field of artificial life was to reinforce the notion that sometimes, all it takes is individual parties abiding by self-interested, myopic rules of behavior to generate the semblance of choreographed activity.

What's compelling about the concept of self-organizing systems is how little they demand of their participants. There are really only two essential requirements for participation in a flock. The first is a sensory apparatus, an awareness of what other parties are doing around you. In business, this is effectively what our competitive positioning maps do for us: They provide us with an awareness of our position relative to others, a hyper-sensitivity to where our closest competitors stand in relation to us.

The second is a predisposition to make the necessary adjustments when nearby parties shift direction. When it comes to flocking, the rules of behavior are fundamentally reactive. What this means is that if nearby birds start drifting to the left, there must be an inclination to follow suit. If they start speeding up to the right, there must be an inclination to follow suit.

In business, not only does this inclination exist, it is ingrained. Our competitive sensory apparatus has conditioned us to not let other companies get too close, but not let them get too far either. So when American Airlines gains a slight edge in the airline industry by introducing a frequent-flier program, or when Colgate gains a slight edge in oral cosmetics by introducing tooth-whitening control, we are keenly aware of the imperative to match pace. More generally, if the competition as a whole appears to be moving in a particular direction, the inclination to drift in the same direction can feel natural to the point of automaticity.

This proclivity to stay with the flock can be particularly pronounced with respect to nearby competitors. Think about it: If Harvard were to offer all of its students a free year abroad, the pressure would be on Yale and Princeton—not the University of Florida—to do likewise. If the Ritz-Carlton were to announce free overnight dry cleaning for all of its guests, the Four Seasons would experience more pressure to match the offer than if Motel 6 were to announce the same. This is why competitive clusters within a category often appear to be moving in such tight lockstep with each other—because conformity is most likely to manifest among groups of competitors that are already the most similar to begin with.

It is also why organic collusion can be so endemic in cutthroat markets. The more tightly contested the category, the more clustered the competition, which means (1) the more hyper-vigilant companies are going to be to the movements of those around them and (2) the more poised they will be to respond in kind. It doesn't take much to see how this kind of ongoing jockeying can quickly become all-consuming; when companies are fighting tooth and nail for every market share point, the relentlessness of this kind of competitive engagement can easily take on a life of its own.

And yet for the individual firm, this meta-dynamic is unlikely to register, for the same reason that drivers stuck in a traffic jam rarely stop to think about their own role in the congestion. As Craig Reynolds's algorithm so elegantly suggests, sometimes the view from the inside out can be very different than the view from the outside in.

It was Irving Janis who in 1972 popularized the term "groupthink" to describe the phenomenon of individuals in a group reaching consensus without a critical testing and evaluation of ideas. The pejorative was in many ways an echo of the social mindset at the time; if you remember, the 1970s were an era in which we viewed collective behavior of any sort—particularly that which carried even a whiff of Orwellian mindlessness—with suspicion. When I was growing up, conformity was an epithet. Peer pressure was an epithet. Mob psychology was an epithet. Even the word "collective" called to mind Soviet-like connotations.

But in the past couple of decades, something has turned. There has been a change in the tenor of our conversation around group behavior. Today, our cultural lexicon is replete with references to a newfound optimism in the benefits of self-organizing systems. Collective intelligence. Smart mobs. The wisdom of crowds. The central conceit in this more recent dialogue is that organic collusion of the sort that arises from intelligent, independent decision making can lead to optimal and even beautiful outcomes.

I raise these two countervailing perspectives, not to argue for the validity of one over the other, but because I believe there's a crux in their reconciliation. The latter view reminds us that there are scenarios in which a single, shared outcome can be beneficial to all. Collective intelligence, collaborative filtering, Wikipedia—in all of these scenarios, it has become evident that unpremeditated collaboration holds the potential to work the kind of wonders that no amount of orchestration could ever match.

The former view reminds us, however, that there are other times when convergence toward a single, shared outcome can leave us with an aftermath that is nothing less than stifling. The critical question comes down to whether in a given situation there is value in diversity, in the emergence of multiple divergent outcomes. When it comes to track-and-field, we may want our runners moving in the same direction, but when it comes to medical care or higher education, we may not.

In business, of course, differentiation is generally considered a firm's primary defense against commoditization. And in theory, the more fierce the competition, the stronger the firm's commitment to differentiation should be. But in fact, I have argued that the opposite is often true: The more diligently firms compete with each other, the less differentiated they can become, at least in the eyes of consumers.

Moreover, the irony is this: To a large extent, the herdlike behaviors I have described in this chapter emanate from what most managers would regard as best practice wisdoms. Know thy competition. Listen to your customers. They tap into characteristics that most managers would regard as best practice traits. Vigilance. Lack of complacency. Responsiveness.

Meanwhile, the very instruments that these managers are relying on to establish and reinforce differentiation—competitive metrics, positioning maps, and customer surveys—have devolved into their obverse. They contribute to the herding behavior as opposed to protect against it. It's as if the entire community has been betrayed by the tools of their trade.

———

So just for the fun of it, let's conjure up a counterfactual. Let's imagine a category in which ten companies were forced to operate blind to what each other was doing. Or to put it more specifically, let's imagine a category in which all ten competitors had to make all of their business decisions—about what to offer, how to innovate, how to price, how to advertise, and so on—without the benefit of knowing where they stood relative to one another. What would be the result?

My prediction is that you'd get ten companies pursuing wildly divergent strategies. Or to use the language of this chapter, ten birds flying off in completely different directions.

Don't get me wrong, I'm not suggesting that businesses should operate this way; I offer the counterfactual to be provocative, not prescriptive. Still, to carry the scenario one step further, what do you think would happen to these companies once they were in flight?

My guess is that while a few would probably crash and burn pretty quickly, a few would probably manage to stay aflight . . . and most important, a couple might even make their way to a place pretty fantastic.

By the same token, as a teacher, I've learned that

when I want to assign my students a large project to complete, there are two ways I can go about it. One way is to give them a list of project benchmarks and to be explicit about the parameters along which they will be evaluated. A second way is to provide them with no explicit benchmarks, no specific parameters for grading—to provide them with nothing more than the understanding that my expectations for their performance will be high.

When I do the first, the results are pretty predictable. At the end of the semester I get a bunch of projects that are safe and conventional, easy to compare against each other, and a cinch to grade. But when I do the second, something different happens. Certainly, I have to spend a good deal of time at the beginning of the semester managing student confusion and uncertainty over the lack of clear guidelines. However, my reward comes at the end of the semester when I am handed a bunch of projects that are different from each other in as many ways as it is possible for them to be different. And although some of these projects invariably miss the mark, most of them turn out just fine . . . and there are always a couple that have managed to find excellence of a sort that I would never have dreamed of asking for in the first place.

━━━

When I think back to my teacher's comments about intelligence, the reason I think I was so frustrated with her responses was that they simply weren't actionable. I wanted to *be* intelligent, and her answers didn't tell me how to get there. What I really wanted, in other words, was an IQ test, along with instructions for how to study for it. I needed a focus for my aspiration.

Fortunately for me, she would have none of it. Because this is what my teacher understood: When it comes to some things—particularly aspirational ideals like intelligence, or quality, or performance, or beauty—we find psychological safety in definitions that are concrete, measurable, and agreed upon.

Take these away, and we will almost certainly experience feelings of dislocation. This is what happens whenever anyone is forced to operate outside of their comfort zone. Yet in the long run, this is not necessarily a bad thing, especially if the objective is not to create a flock of obedient followers, but to sustain a divergence of unconstrained thinking.

As a teacher, when you refuse to put a box around some abstract vision of achievement, when you refuse to impose a measuring tape against which that achievement can be measured, you are in many ways coaxing your students to constructively rebel. You are encouraging them to consider the meaning of excellence absent the authority of an exogenous metric, and you are giving them license to surprise you—and perhaps even surprise themselves—with what they come up with.

the paradox
of progress

On the day I became a parent, I lost the ability to get stuck in a moment. When I was a child, the only moment I ever paid attention to was the one I was in. Summer was a ceaseless stretch of lazy days filled with nothingness. I was eight years old for a lifetime. I was nine years old for a lifetime. I turned ten, and that year lasted a lifetime, too.

But to be a parent is to live in the past-present-future all at once. It is to hug your children and be intensely aware of how much smaller they felt last year . . . even as you wonder how much bigger they will feel the next. It is to be a time-shifter, to marvel at the budding of their intellect, their verbal dexterity, their sense of humor . . . at the same time rewinding and fast-forwarding . . . to when they were younger, to when they'll be older. It is to experience longing for the here and now, which I know sounds flaky—sort of like complaining about being homesick when you're already home—but can happen, trust me, when you live in multiple time zones all at once.

To be a parent is to be the caretaker of your children's past and future at an age when they cannot possibly fathom that either matters. When I hear people say that time moves faster as you get older, I think they have it wrong. It's not that time moves any faster; it's that time collapses altogether.

———

Relative to my own upbringing, there are things that I find different about my children's lives and things that I find are the same, and at the risk of over-generalizing, they sort of boil down to this: The trappings have changed, but the plot hasn't much. My sons play capture-the-flag on a manicured lawn groomed with animal-safe weed killer, but they still play capture-the-flag. They write their school reports on laptops and leave messages on my cell, but they still do their homework and check in with Mom. The paradox of time, of progress, of evolution has always been this: *plus ça change, plus c'est la même chose*—the more things change, the more things stay the same. It is the internal contradiction of a movie remake: the actors are new, and the props and set design have been updated, but the story line is intimately familiar.

My younger son recently discovered an old Hanna-Barbera television sitcom called *The Jetsons;* it aired in the 1960s and featured a cartoon family living in an animated futuristic world. What's interesting about the show is what's interesting about science fiction in general: Nothing and everything is the same. George Jetson goes to work in a flying saucer with a transparent top, but he still goes to work every day. Han Solo walks into a bar and it's a weird-looking joint with weird-looking dudes, but he's still just looking for a drink. You can play this game forward and backward: Fred Flintstone is a prehistoric caveman living in the Stone Age, but he still teases his wife and hangs with his pal Barney. The nouns and objects have changed, but the verbs have not.

And yet to sum this up by saying that people don't change but the stuff around them does is not quite right, either. Like many parents, when I want to impress upon my children how well I sympathize with whatever internal up or down they're going through, I will offer them a story from my own adolescence in which the emotional parallels are obvious.

But when I want to impress upon them how fortunate they are, how appreciative they should be for the richness of their lives, it's hard not to point to the stuff around them. And so the narratives I offer in this context are ones in which the material contrasts are explicit. It's a well-worn parental tactic, I know— forcing your kids to endure vivid descriptions of the dusty articles of your youth: typewriters, slide rules, telephone booths, and cassette players. And yet it's a revealing tactic as well, for what you are implicitly telling your children is that as the things around them change, they *do* change, too, or at least the quality of their existence does.

Every time my husband tosses another load in the laundry while I order our groceries online, we are compressing a day's worth of our parents' old to-do list into fifteen minutes of our own. Multiply those extra hours against the entirety of our adulthood, and you'll see why we are able to give more time to each other and our children than our parents ever could. My first car accident occurred a few years back, and when it did, the air bag came at me so instantaneously that it wasn't until afterward that it occurred to me to consider the role the car itself had played in keeping me safe. When the stuff around us transforms, we are transformed, too, and we are often better off as a result.

This is why, when it comes to progress and evolution, we are optimists, and who can blame us? Sure, we recognize that progress tends to happens slowly and incrementally, with one advance laying the foundation for the next, but we also know that sometimes, the cumulative sum of those incremental improvements can pay out exponential dividends.

We are all time-shifters in this regard. We buy a house because we know it'll look great if we just add a bathroom here, change the wallpaper there. We take a job because we anticipate an easy path to promotion. In each of these cases, we envision the future, and when we do, we envision the future perfect.

─ⱶ─

And yet this still doesn't quite get it right. Sometimes the future comes at us in a way that makes us want to recoil. The first time my husband reentered a toy store after having ignored them for a couple of decades, he came home dismayed at what modernity had wrought: Gone were the wooden Tinkertoy sets and charming playthings of his youth, only to be replaced with newfangled gizmos and weird blinking electronica. I suppose that some of his dismay could be explained by nostalgia, except that nostalgia itself is a funny concept—optimism facing the wrong direction, almost.

When you recuse yourself from a product category for a number of years only to find yourself plunged back into it at some later point in time, the experience can be off-putting, if not disenchanting. Try shopping for a new washing machine, a new home entertainment system, a new microwave, a new toy set for your kid—if you haven't done so in a while, you're in for a jolt.

As a genre, science fiction does this routinely, to dramatic effect—it shoves us into a world in which change hasn't had a chance to creep up on us. This is when we realize that while product evolution can appear marvelous in its incarnation, it can also appear puzzling, pointless, even absurd. *Why would the Jetsons want to live in an airtight glass bubble? Why would anyone want to eat their meals in pill form?* Of course, our ancestors could have voiced the same doubts about us: *Why would anyone want to live in apartment boxes stacked on top of each other? Why would anyone want to get their vitamins and nutrients in pill form?* But we sheepishly know this already, which explains at least part of our ambivalence toward the physical artifacts of our existence.

Change is good; change is bad; tomorrow can't come fast enough; slow tomorrow down. There is an inconsistency here, a lack of order to our logic. We size up the future and we're optimistic; we're pessimistic. We're eager; we're disenchanted. Most of all, we're demanding, unreasonably so—which is to say, we want what we want, right here right now, and we want it exactly the way we want it, no different, and nothing more.

Personally speaking, I hate that TV remote controls have gotten more complicated than scientific calculators, and it irks me to no end that my current laptop takes twice as long to boot up as my last one. I miss ice cream trucks, analog alarm clocks, and LPs. On the other hand, I couldn't live without air-conditioning, online newspapers, and my Kindle.

So maybe this still doesn't get it quite right. It's not that we're demanding of the future; it's that we're unforgiving. We put our faith in the promise of progress . . . but if it just so happens that the future gets it a little bit wrong, we can be disappointed to the point of disillusion.

⁓

This is where product marketers differ from consumers.

Where consumers are inconsistent in their attitude toward progress, product marketers are consistent. Where consumers are ambivalent in their regard for change, product marketers are unambivalent. And where consumers are fickle in their posture toward product evolution, product marketers are predictable. Remarkably predictable. Extraordinarily predictable.

And while this may sound like a reproach, it really isn't intended to be. If you were to visit a typical consumer products firm, my guess is you'd be pleasantly surprised at how genuinely customer-focused the people who work there are. It's a refreshing thing to encounter, particularly if you're someone who has it in your head that all business folk are calculating cynics out to cheat people out of their money. Nothing could be further from the truth.

More specifically, if you were to observe business professionals in action across a spectrum of consumer markets—from automobiles to hotels to beverages to detergent—what you'd find is that when they talk about product evolution, most of them are notably straightforward in their intentions: They simply want to make their products better. They'll typically use the term "product augmentation" to refer to this objective, and more often than not, it'll take one of two forms.

The first is what I like to call *augmentation-by-addition*. To the extent that a product (or a "value proposition") can be thought of as a set of benefits, product marketers will habitually look to improve it by bolstering those benefits. Sometimes they'll do this by strengthening an already-existing benefit—say, by boosting the stain-fighting ability of their detergent, or by extending the length of their warranty; other times, they'll do it by slapping on a new feature or benefit—by adding fabric softener to that detergent, or a money-back guarantee to that warranty. In any event, when businesses engage in augmentation-by-addition, the idea is to please customers by giving them what they expect, plus more:

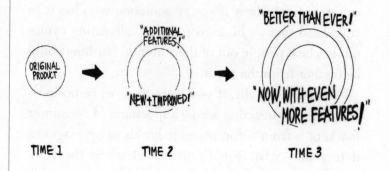

Examples of augmentation-by-addition can be found everywhere, in every conceivable category. It used to be that toothpaste offered the singular promise of cavity-free teeth; today, toothpaste offers the additional promises of fresh breath, tartar control, and a whiter smile. It used to be that laundry detergent offered the singular promise of clean clothes; today, there is static elimination, stain protection, and fabric softening. In each of these cases, the value proposition has gotten bigger and bigger over time.

The second form of product augmentation is what I like to call *augmentation-by-multiplication*. Because companies recognize that different people have different preferences, they'll frequently hatch specialized versions of their product in an attempt to meet the needs of specific consumer segments. Instead of selling Coke, they'll sell Diet Coke, Cherry Coke, Caffeine-Free Coke, and Diet Coke with Lemon. Here, the idea is to increase the likelihood of satisfying consumers by offering them a portfolio of products to choose from, each of which consists of a core set of benefits combined with segment-specific augmentations:

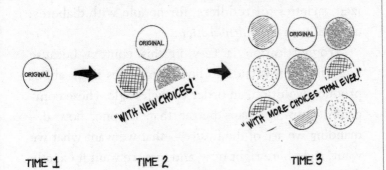

AUGMENTATION-BY-MULTIPLICATION

ORIGINAL → ORIGINAL "WITH NEW CHOICES!" → ORIGINAL "WITH MORE CHOICES THAN EVER!"

TIME 1   TIME 2   TIME 3

You see augmentation-by-multiplication in every conceivable category, too. It used to be that if you wanted to purchase a pencil, you'd be stuck buying a simple number 2. Your choices today would fill an entire aisle in your local office supply store.

Again, in both types of augmentation, the objective is the same: to make the product better, in either a cumulative or a reproductive fashion. One of the assignments I like to give my students requires that they choose an established product category and predict what it'll look like in five to ten years. When they hand in their predictions, the two themes that crop up again and again are augmentation-by-addition and augmentation-by-multiplication. Computers will come with more memory, more storage capacity: *augmentation-by-addition*. Computers will come in specialized versions for children, for the elderly: *augmentation-by-multiplication*. Cereal will come in easier-to-open boxes with easier-to-open inner bags: *augmentation-by-addition*. Cereal will come in special- ized varieties for toddlers, for people with diabetes: *augmentation-by-multiplication*.

Prognostication is easy in this context because there is a consistency to how companies think about product evolution, an order to their logic. These com- panies know, perhaps better than anyone, how de- manding we are of the future—that we want what we want, right here right now, and that we want it exactly the way we want it, no different, and nothing more. And so they try to give it to us the best way they know how. It should come as no wonder then, that in cate- gory after category, product evolution tends to take on these two predictable trajectories.

In 1999, Westin Hotels decided to augment its value proposition by introducing The Heavenly Bed—ten layers of sumptuous, custom-designed sleeping ex- travagance. I'm not kidding when I say that the first time I tried one of these beds I caught a squint of the hereafter; the bed was just that delicious.

But although I was grateful for the good night's sleep, the truth is I spent very little time reflecting on the amount of business energy that went into produc- ing this particular augmentation. When a company commits itself to product improvement, the investment will often require the mobilization of multiple functions within the company—marketing, engineering, operations, new product development. It apparently took Westin Hotels more than a year and $30 million to develop The Heavenly Bed; the company tested literally hundreds of mattresses, pillows, and linens in the process.

A few years back, *The New Yorker* ran an article that detailed the relentless intensity with which disposable diaper manufacturers—Kimberly-Clark, which produces Huggies, and Procter & Gamble, which produces Pampers—endeavor to improve the absorbency and compactness of what is essentially a throwaway sponge. What made the story compelling was that it offered a voyeuristic peek into the strange, obsessive microcosm that these companies call home. Acquisition layers, re-wet tests, polymer components—it was impossible to get through the article without feeling somewhat humbled by the seriousness, rigor, and ferocity with which these firms contemplate diaper augmentation.

Most consumers know that a company such as Intel will routinely deploy vast resources to enhance the performance of its computer chips. What they don't know is that a similar degree of dedication is equally likely to reside in businesses that produce canned soup, oatmeal raisin cookies, and household cleaners. When my sons play capture-the-flag in our front yard, they enjoy the advantages of the weed-free and pet-safe environment, but the focused commitment that went into producing these advantages is thoroughly imperceptible to them.

I took the boys to the beach on a recent Saturday and this is how the scene unfolded: They began the day by throwing a few fruit-flavored vitamin-enhanced-water bottles into their kid-sized, water-resistant backpacks. They applied sunblock and mosquito repellent, and then hit the water sporting quick-dry rash shirts, goggles, and waterproof sandals. After a full day in the scorching sun, they returned home—fully hydrated, with no sunburn or bug bites, with nary a scratch on their feet, having gotten 100 percent of their recommended daily allowance of vitamins and minerals. When the stuff around us transforms, there's no question we can be better off as a result.

Of course, this is not to say that companies are altruistic in their commitment to product augmentation; when a firm decides to improve its product, it does so for any number of business reasons—to increase revenues, to grow the brand, to promote loyalty, to expand the category, and so on. The people who run these companies aren't saints, nor do they owe it to us to be.

It is simply to say that the business of pushing progress can be a thankless one. Whenever you hear someone proclaim, "I've decided to wait until next year before I buy a new X because I know the Xs next year will be so much better," what you are hearing is someone articulate what we all take for granted: When it comes to product evolution, we leave it to firms to deliver the future perfect, and we're complacent in the knowledge that *they* know we expect it of them, too.

—————

About thirty years ago, Philip Brickman, a social psychologist at Northwestern University, organized a team of researchers to investigate the happiness levels of lottery winners. The team found that while lottery winners were initially elated upon landing their great fortune, those feelings of elation tended to dissipate rapidly. As the winners recalibrated their happiness levels, many of the activities they had previously enjoyed (such as reading or sitting down to a good meal) became less pleasurable over time, such that within a few months, the wealthy winners reported being no happier than they had been before hitting the jackpot. Brickman called this adaptational phenomenon the "hedonic treadmill"; the term was dead on in describing the human predisposition to feel entitled to today what we used to feel thankful for yesterday.

What's amusing about so many of the studies on hedonic adaptation is that they demonstrate the extent to which our propensity to become spoiled is, from an evolutionary perspective, practically a foregone conclusion. For example, in another study, Daniel Kahneman (a social psychologist and Nobel laureate) and his colleague Jackie Snell confirmed what most of us intuitively know—that if you give people a treat too often, they become less appreciative of it over time.

Specifically, the researchers found that if you give peo-ple a portion of their favorite ice cream for eight days in a row, they end up liking it less. Again, when it comes to our consumption experiences, we seem to move from being delighted to being blasé in the blink of an eye.

This propensity is most easily painted in the jux-taposition of times and contexts. Whether it be the Flintstones, the Jetsons, the Ingalls, or the Huxta-bles—the trappings may change, but our content-ment doesn't much. When Voltaire said "happiness is an illusion; only suffering is real," he may as well have been referring to the futility of Freud's pleasure principle.

And yet this is precisely why, for the businessper-son, it can be useful to be a time-shifter. Consider how augmentation-by-addition would appear, revis-ited through the lens of collapsed sequential motion:

1. A company augments its value proposition by offering consumers a new benefit.
2. Customers are pleased.
3. Competitors race to match (imitate) the aug-mentation.
4. The augmentation becomes standard across the category.
5. Satisfaction levels are recalibrated, which is to say that customers now feel entitled to what they were grateful for yesterday.
6. Meanwhile, the expected value proposition has

expanded and the minimal requirements for competing in the category have gone up.

7. Repeat step 1.

If this were a plot, not only would it be recurring, it would play on multiple channels: American Airlines augments its value proposition by introducing a frequent-flier program. Customers are pleased. Competitors race to match (imitate) the augmentation. Frequent-flier programs become standard across the industry. The entire category is back to where it started, with the exception that the ante has been raised—meaning it has become more costly for firms to compete in the category.

Viewed from this perspective, it could be argued that product augmentation is but an expensive route to commoditization—the more generous the standard value proposition becomes within the category, the easier it becomes for consumers to be indifferent to which competitive alternative they choose. Once consumers realize that all airlines offer frequent-flier programs, that all detergents offer enhanced stain fighting, that all companies offer good warranties, they have less reason to be picky in their selections.

The plot transpires with a slight twist in the case of augmentation-by-multiplication. Here is how the bottled water category would appear if you were to rewind back to a few years ago:

THEN

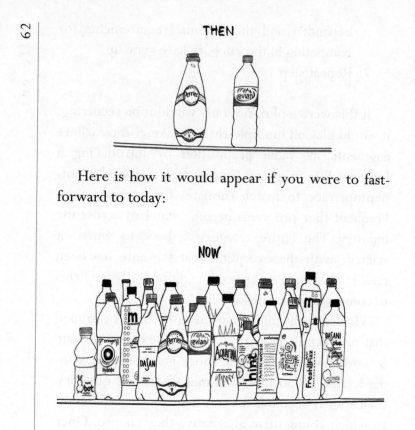

Here is how it would appear if you were to fast-forward to today:

NOW

This is the business world's version of mitosis—a single-celled organism splitting and reproducing, again and again and again. Here is how the Post-it Note category would appear if you were to rewind back to a few years ago:

THEN

Here is how it would appear if you were to fast-forward to today:

NOW

Whenever you see this kind of heterogeneous homogeneity—a multiplication of products and brands competing across a multiplication of subsegments—what you are witnessing is hyper-segmentation in action. You are watching companies slice-and-dice a market into smaller and smaller subsegments in a persistent attempt to root out overlooked consumer pockets.

However, you are also seeing how it is possible to micro-segment a market to the point of common senselessness. *Would you prefer a low-calorie premium dark lager, or a dark premium light ale? A mid-distance running shoe, or a short-distance low-impact cross-trainer?* This is the stage at which the category starts to conjure the worst of two worlds—a growing profusion of alternatives, a shrinking proportion of which are meaningful. Product augmentation has become, once again, an expensive route to commoditization.

What is perhaps most disheartening about this phenom-enon is how skillful businesses have become at sustaining it. In recent years, this art—the art of relentless, incre-mental augmentation, whether by addition or by multi-plication—has become an essential product marketing competency; it has become what modern marketers *do*.

I recently conducted some field research on the bottled water industry and spent a good deal of time listening to industry executives explain what made their water different from that of their competitors. Take a look at how the managers at VOSS, a super-premium water brand, describe the unique merits of their water in their marketing materials:

> VOSS Artesian Water comes from an aquifer in the pristine nature of Southern Norway, pro-tected from pollutants by layers of rock and sand, producing a pure water unlike any other.
>
> When tapped into, the aquifer is pressurized enough to allow the water to rise up naturally through the ground without the use of mechani-cal pumps. Because the water is protected by this impermeable layer, it does not come into contact with the air or other pollutants.

Now look at how the folks at FIJI, a competitive water brand, describe the unique merits of theirs:

> Preserved and protected by its source and loca-tion, FIJI Water's aquifer is in a virgin ecosystem

at the edge of a primitive rainforest, a continent away from the nearest industrialized civilization. Our rainfall is purified by equatorial winds after traveling thousands of miles across the Pacific Ocean. Winds that carry acid rain and pollutants to other parts of the planet just don't come our way. So if you ever wondered what really pure water tastes like, just open a bottle of FIJI Water.

Whew.

Notice the excessive elaboration in these descriptions. In my mind, this is a bizarre strain of business expertise at play, and when product marketing begins to take on this form, it's not only the claims of augmentation that begin to lose credence but the claims of differentiation as well. Both Huggies and Pampers claim to sell products that are augmented, but they also claim to sell products that are augmented in different ways from each other. Pampers Baby-Dry Diapers, for example, come with "caterpillar flex"—extraflexible tabs that expand and contract with your baby—while Huggies Snug & Dry come with an all-around stretch for a super-snug fit to allow your baby to explore their world. Pampers Baby-Dry have an "UltraAbsorb™ Core"; Huggies Snug & Dry have "LeakLock® protection." Pampers Baby-Dry feature Elmo from *Sesame Street* on every diaper; Huggies Snug & Dry feature Mickey Mouse.

Here again, whatever incongruities exist, exist only in the fine print. The devil, as they say, is in the details. And yet in too many cases, this is what business has been reduced to: the artful packaging of meaning-less distinctions as true differentiation.

—*mm*—

In 1980, Ted Levitt—a business scholar widely re-garded as one of most influential marketing minds of his generation—published a now-classic polemic enti-tled "Marketing Success Through Differentiation . . . of Anything." In the article, Levitt challenged busi-nesses to establish points of differentiation in the most unlikely of places; market share points could be won or lost, Levitt convincingly argued, on the basis of competitive divergence in areas that companies had historically neglected to consider.

And yet reading the article several decades after its publication, it's hard not to come to the conclusion that business has taken Levitt's challenge to a self-defeating extreme. It's almost as if companies have be-come *too* facile at squeezing differentiation out of minuscule discrepancies; they have gotten *too* adept at making mountains out of molehills.

Consider: When Gillette introduced its classic Blue Blade razor in 1930, it waited more than forty years before introducing its first upgrade, the Trac II, with its twin blades. It waited another eighteen years before introducing the Sensor, but then took only five years to launch the Sensor Excel. The time to its next product extension, the Mach3 (with three blades in-stead of two), was just four years. This was almost im-mediately followed by at least four extensions, including the Mach3Turbo and the Mach3Power

Nitro. Most of these products are still on the market, sold alongside Gillette's newest model, the five-blade Fusion, which—despite its relative newness to the product line—already has a number of incarnations: the Fusion Power, the Fusion Phenom, and the Fusion Power Phenom.

Another example: It took Coca-Cola nearly a century (ninety-six years, to be precise) to introduce its first product extension, Diet Coke. Today, Coca-Cola sells more than a dozen versions of its brand—including Coke Zero, Vanilla Coke, Diet Coke with Lime, Diet Coke Sweetened with Splenda, and Diet Coke Plus (fortified with vitamins and minerals)—and introduces new brand extensions on an almost routine basis.

In other words, it used to be the case that change happened slowly and steadily, with one advance carefully laying the foundation for the next. But in an increasing number of industries, change now happens quickly and indiscriminately, in such a way that the cumulative sum of those augmentations doesn't seem to pay out much at all. In my mind, this is the mark of a category that has lost its discipline.

I use the term "hyper-maturity" to refer to this stage of category evolution; it's the stage at which all of the hyper-segmentation, hyper-augmentation, and competitive hyper-activity within the category starts to appear as a bit of a blur. Incidentally, when I find myself plunged into a category in which change itself has become a commodity, this is when I see the future looking at me in a way that makes me want to recoil.

Here, then, is The Heavenly Bed story, recast through the prism of collapsed time:

In the years that followed Westin's introduction of The Heavenly Bed, Hilton announced the introduction of its own Serenity Bed in all of its properties. Marriott invested roughly $190 million to replace all of its bedding with its Revive Collection. Hyatt rolled out its Hyatt Grand Bed, Radisson introduced its Sleep Number Bed, and Crowne Plaza launched a Sleep Advantage program. In short, the hotel bed wars became a case study in competitive one-upsmanship.

I stay in hotels quite a bit, and I have to say, the last time I stayed in a hotel in D.C., I needed a stepstool to climb past the mountain of mattress pads, comforters, duvet covers, pillows, and bolsters covering the monstrosity of a bed monopolizing my room. Occasionally, I'll experience a moment when I'm embarrassed to be living in the twenty-first century, and this was one of them.

A few years ago, *The Onion* ran an article describing Coca-Cola's launch of a new 30-liter bottle weighing 274 pounds, standing four feet tall, and requiring three men to lift. Humor is only funny when it's rooted in some fundamental reality, and what made this particular gag amusing was that it captured the fundamental reality of product augmentation: It never stops, even when it should.

There comes a point beyond which we are hard to impress. There comes a point beyond which additional improvement ceases to add value. When we hear that someone very skinny has decided to go on a diet, or that someone healthy and beautiful has decided to get plastic surgery, we will have any number of reactions, none of which are approving. Why? Because we know that there comes a point beyond which further augmentation reveals nothing more than a lack of judgment.

—⁓—

Whenever I teach in one of the many executive education programs offered by my school, I will often include a lecture on the characteristics of hyper-mature categories. I'll describe the phenomenon of competitive herding, and I'll lay out the dynamics associated with relentless, incremental augmentation. I'll discuss satisfaction treadmills and the proliferation of dissimilar clones. And I'll offer many, many examples: The laundry detergent category is a hyper-mature category. The sneaker category is a hyper-mature category. The cellular industry is a hyper-mature category.

And I'll talk about how the winner in all of these categories should be consumers—partly because the products within them have gotten better over time (augmentation-by-addition), and partly because there are more product choices to be had (augmentation-by-multiplication)—but I'll also describe how the reality is a lot more complicated than this. In so many of these categories, overall customer satisfaction levels haven't budged much at all over the years. Indeed, it's been a good forty-some years since Mick Jagger busted out on the radio singing, "I'm watchin' my TV and that man comes on to tell me . . . how white my shirts can be." Yet as consumers, we *still* can't seem to get no satisfaction.

What this means is that these are categories in which companies are literally running to stand still. This, in fact, is a telltale sign that a category has achieved hyper-maturity: Overall growth in the category has slowed to a trickle even as the competitive hyper-activity in the category has become more frenzied than ever.

If the whole exercise sounds exhausting it's because it is, and believe me, the executives in my classroom feel that exhaustion and they're not shy about saying so. At the same time, they're remarkably candid about the fact that they feel resigned to the competitive dynamic they find themselves caught up in. Some of them go so far as to argue that the dynamic that I've described is all just part of the rough-and-tumble jockeying that makes the business world go 'round.

Perhaps you agree. If so, my response tends to be rather long-winded, so I've devoted a later section of this book to go into it in greater detail. For now, let me simply say this.

What's rough about being a businessperson is that it's easy to get stuck in a moment. When you find yourself mired in the unrelenting tussle of competitive skirmish, it's easy to forget that the moment you are in has a history and a future. Some may be better than none. But more may not be better than some, and more-more-more may not be any good at all; when you are stuck in a moment, it's easy to forget this.

This is why, in business, it can be useful to be a time-shifter. Because if you happen to be someone who operates in the past-present-future all at once, you're likely to see how an overabundance of positives could eventually give birth to a negative. You're likely to see how the ceaselessness of the customer satisfaction treadmill could eventually become a recipe for madness. And you're likely to see how the line separating the future perfect and the future imperfect can be tenuous indeed.

The paradox of progress is that it makes things better, until it makes things worse.

So if I have one piece of advice for you, for the time being, anyway, it is this. Play the story backward and play the story forward. Rewind, fast-forward, last year, next year. And try to envision your market through the lens of alternative future possibilities.

the category blur
(how we cope)

it used to be that self-disclosure was a bit of a dance—I share a little bit about myself, you share a little bit back. I share a little more, you share a bit back. Getting to know someone took not just time but reciprocity; there was a delicate mutuality to the exchange. I peel back a layer. Now you. Now me. Now you. And with each new revelation, there emerged first, acquaintance, then familiarity, and finally, intimacy.

But the internet has changed this somehow. Go online and you'll see what I mean. Match.com, Facebook, Flickr, YouTube . . . In the aggressive world of hyper-connectivity, self-disclosure is no longer conditioned on reciprocity; it is unilateral, unsolicited, offered up for free. To write a blog is to engage in a public confessional. To sign up for Facebook is to host a coming-out party for yourself. It's almost as if technology has unleashed the exhibitionist in all of us.

And apparently, nothing is out of bounds, not even the mundane. Twitter has millions of members who go out of their way to keep the world up to date on the quotidian details of their every waking minute. Consider some of these recent posts:

" . . . I find that beer consumption rises during major home projects. Same with foul language, of course."

" . . . In this digital age, am I the only adult still writing on my hand?"

" . . . Hour and a half of cardio, Lean Cuisine for lunch, mail shows up, see son's math grade, eat giant handful of M&Ms. Emotional eating much?"

This is kinetic terrain, hypnotic in its coolness and elasticity, but disorienting, too, in the fearlessness of its citizenry. Here's a look at a profile from MySpace:

About Me: Music is my true love. Rock, indie, acoustic, alternative, reggae, and punk, mostly. My only enemy is country music. I'm obsessed with making art. Love to draw, love to paint. I'm not sure what color eyes I have. Honestly, it changes. Usually blue-ish though. I hate hypocrites, but think that everyone is one in their own way. I don't like talking about people behind their backs. I quote movies in my daily conversations.

When all the world's a stage, everything becomes a study in impression management; everything becomes the modern-day answer to the question *What do I want the world to think of me?* Which is partly why the internet has become such a treasure trove for business—it's become the place where citizens congregate to market themselves to the world.

⌇

Imagine if every day, every one of us had to go to work wearing a magical T-shirt that listed everything we had seen on television over the previous twenty-four-hours—every reality show, every god-awful sitcom, every piece of dreck that we hadn't planned on watching but ended up sitting through anyway—every dreadful detail would be unveiled to our coworkers upon our arrival at the office the next day. Imagine how quickly our television viewing habits would change. Imagine how much less TV we'd watch. Imagine how much more judicious we'd be flipping through the channels knowing that all of our selections were destined to become public knowledge.

When we move from private to public consumption what changes is our attentiveness. When we're alone, we can afford to be careless in our consumption and so we tend to be. But once we know that people are watching, we're apt to pay a bit more attention, sometimes quite a bit more, because now we know that everything we do, everything we wear, everything we eat holds the potential to become a window into who we are. And so we monitor our consumption in ways that we wouldn't otherwise. We change our clothes before leaving the house. We're careful about what we drink when dining with the boss. Even when we choose to disregard protocol—when we opt to wear our most ratty jeans to a formal dinner party, for example—we do so self-consciously, flagrantly even. Consumption becomes a performance in every sense of the word.

Nowhere is this more apparent than in the virtual republic that is web nation. To be an accidental tourist in this land is not unlike stumbling into a global game of show-and-tell: Consumption is shorthand for identity; people reveal who they are by revealing what they consume.

Take this Facebook excerpt:

> Interests: I love tattoos, Range Rovers, the Red Sox, iPhone, UGGs, working out, drinkin' girly drinks, Papyrus cards, JUICY COUTURE ♥, Sephora, being tan, Hudson jeans, and Britney Spears.

What you're seeing here is an inversion of the old advertising formula—brands used to describe actors instead of the other way around. And while it's easy to underestimate the forethought that goes into constructing these online compositions, when you browse through Facebook or Match.com or Twitter, what you need to remember is that every word on every page has been put there for a reason: to sculpt your impression of the person you are reading about. A posted declaration such as "I couldn't live without my caffeine and my Converse All-Stars," is seldom as offhand as it appears. Indeed, when it comes to the performance art known as social networking, it can sometimes feel as if there's nothing *but* marketing going on—people playing publicist, working for themselves.

Try it. Go online. Look carefully. Consumption has become the identity cloak of our generation.

—————

In the town in which I live, the magical age at which kids begin picking up the patois of stylized consumption seems to occur around the fifth or sixth grade. This is when you see girls refusing to wear jeans unless they're Hollisters, when you see boys rejecting Reeboks in favor of Vans. It's a curious sight to behold; hordes of preteens experimenting with their identities by alternately adopting and rejecting the consumptive slang of their peers. Of course, they morph into ridiculously picky shoppers in the process. (Any parent who's ever gone clothes shopping with their sixteen-year-old knows what I'm talking about.) And yet there doesn't seem to be much a parent can do to stop the process; apparently, the puberty gods are capable of unleashing a bunch of consumption hormones in addition to the sexual ones.

Not all kids go through this phase at the same time or to the same extent. But I personally believe that most of us go through some version of it at one time or another. By the time we reach adulthood, most of us are picky about *something*. Maybe it's the type of golf clubs we prefer or the type of car we drive or the type of makeup we insist upon wearing; most of us are picky about something.

And from a business standpoint, it's a critical phase because if no one ever went through it, the marketing functions of most companies would cease to have reason to exist. Think about it. Nike spent roughly $2 billion on marketing and advertising last year, predicated on the belief that we can be made to become choosy about what we wear to the gym. Procter & Gamble spent more than $5 billion on advertising, predicated on the belief that we can be made to develop a preference for one household product over another.

You could even boil down the entire function of marketing to this—the process by which businesses try to make us picky about what we consume. The process itself is marked by a set of complex business tactics, sure, but the objective itself is remarkably straightforward.

And how do marketing managers know when they are succeeding? One obvious way is by looking at sales data—by looking at how many of us are buying their products. The problem is that this won't necessarily provide a full picture of our consumption attitudes. You and I may be actively purchasing the same brand, but this doesn't mean we are assigning the same meaning to our patronage. You may be consuming out of routine or even reluctance while I am consuming out of passion. In that event, I'm probably more committed to the brand than you are, which is another way of saying that I'm probably less likely to be tempted by competitive offerings.

This is why, in addition to poring over sales data, marketing managers pay so much attention to our public displays of brand affection—to which brands we're wearing, to which brands we're posting on our websites, to which brands we're recommending to each other. Anytime we're willing to publicize our brand affinity to the rest of the world, our connection to the brand is likely to be pretty robust, and marketers know this.

From the perspective of a brand manager, an even better scenario is one in which our brand passion is married to a second ingredient: a belief that the brand delivers something that other brands do not, a belief that derives from obvious comparative diligence. A statement such as "I die for Brigham's mint chocolate chip ice cream" could be considered a sturdy declaration of brand loyalty for two reasons: The extreme fervor in the statement implies passion, while the extreme specificity in the statement implies comparative expertise, an astuteness with respect to the particular benefits of Brigham's mint chocolate chip versus any other brand.

Note that this comparative expertise doesn't necessarily have to have an objective, functional, or even rational basis. When my fashionista assistant insists on wearing only Hugo Boss shoes and Prada sunglasses, and drinking only Grey Goose vodka, his fastidiousness may be based on highly subjective notions about the advantages of these brands versus their competition. No matter. His selectivity is still anchored in an informed awareness of his alternatives, which means that his brand loyalties are rooted in differentiated benefits that are very real to him.

In sum, when these two ingredients—passion and comparative expertise—yield a particular brand preference, they become tenacious in their combination for the express reason that they add up to a sense of irreplaceability. If you're a brand manager, this is precisely what you want—people who not only love your brand but feel that it's the *only* brand able to deliver what they're looking for.

⁓

That said, there are few things I feel certain about when it comes to business, but one of them is that brand loyalty is becoming harder to come by. Yes, I know, I've just spent the past few pages describing the myriad ways in which consumers express their brand affections—in the school yards, on the pages of Facebook—so how can this be?

Well, it's not that I believe brand loyalty is altogether dead; it clearly isn't. As I said, most folks are picky about something—my assistant loves his Pradas; the kids in my town love their Hollisters. It's just that brand loyalty seems to have become more elusive than ever. The phenomenon seems particularly apparent once you begin eliminating some of the flashier categories—fashion, shoes, accessories, etc.—around which people tend to focus their most high-profile consumption activity. Take these away, and you're really not left with much loyalty at all, at least that I can observe.

In fact, I would wager that for most people, the number of categories in which they feel no fidelity toward any particular brand far outnumbers the number of categories in which they do; I would also wager that the balance is tipping further with each passing day. There are literally dozens of brands competing for my affection in categories such as hotels and retail banking and energy bars, for example, and I feel loyalty to exactly zero of them. The teenagers in my town are bombarded with choices with respect to the kinds of juices they drink and the foods they eat, and the vast majority of these brands manage to garner a faddish passing interest at best.

Maybe my recollection is hazy, but it doesn't seem like it was always this way. When I was a kid, my parents' devotion to a mainstay set of brands spanned our entire household inventory. We were a Coke family (no Pepsi). When we bought whipped cream, it was always Cool Whip. My mother swore by Oil of Olay. Herbal Essence shampoo. Lemon-scented Palmolive. My dad swore by Sony televisions. Craftsman tools. Schwinn bicycles. One of my old boyfriends used to consider himself a pretty classy fellow because he always insisted on Häagen-Dazs.

This species of brand loyalty seems almost quaint today. Again, I'm talking about the kind of devotion that families used to routinely bestow upon the everyday stuff that held their lives together. It is this strain of brand affiliation that I believe is dying a slow death.

And evidently, I am not the only one who thinks so. I attended a marketing conference recently where the notion that consumers have lost the inclination to be brand loyal was one of the focal points of discussion. There was a lot of speculation about the possible reasons—the fragmentation of marketing channels, the fickleness of consumers, and so on. But there was little disagreement about the underlying premise.

—————

To be sure, there have always been certain categories that have been considered to be naturally and inherently incompatible with brand loyalty. Two types of categories come to mind here: (1) categories in which there is no obvious brand variety, such as sugar or bond paper or gas stations, and (2) categories in which there is almost infinite variety, such as restaurants or wine or books. You rarely even hear businesspeople talk about brand loyalty in the context of these markets since both of these properties—a lack of brand variety and too much variety—create situations in which loyalty is difficult to sustain.

And yet the predicament of categories that have reached a stage of hyper-maturity is that they can degenerate into markets in which both of these properties coexist. I alluded to this point earlier; cereal can be described as a category in which all the brands are different or all the brands are the same, depending on your point of view. So can sneakers. Or bottled water.

My mother never had to choose a credit card affiliation out of a deluge of credit card offers in her mailbox. She never had to pledge allegiance to a single brand of yogurt out of a vast and constantly rotating selection of yogurts. It's easy to be a Häagen-Dazs loyalist when Häagen-Dazs is the only major player in the premium ice cream game; when the market is packed with premium clones, Häagen-Dazs loyalists are by definition going to be harder to find. My husband and I routinely disregard brands across an array of categories ranging from shampoo to dishwashing soap, to an extent that our parents would never have dreamed of. And it's not because we're all that different than they were, but because we're making our purchases in a very different market context.

Once the dual dynamics of competitive herding and competitive hyper-activity begin to dominate a category, the category itself starts to become incompatible with brand devotion. I really believe this to be true. This is what I mean when I say that brand loyalty is becoming harder to come by. What I'm saying is that when I look around me, I see too many firms in too many categories engaged in precisely the kind of competitive cycle that tends to preclude its emergence.

—————

To be a little more precise, two things tend to happen to consumers once a market reaches hyper-maturity. First, from the perspective of the consumer, all of the hyper-activity within the market begins to appear as a blur. If you recall from an earlier chapter, the signature characteristic of a herd in action is the optical illusion: Not only does the collective appear to have achieved a life of its own, but the illusion has the effect of obscuring individual-level behaviors. The same perceptual transference applies to this context: The category begins to take on an identity of its own that obscures the identities of the individual brands within it.

I watched the football game with my husband the other day and saw a dozen different beer commercials all reinforcing the same masculine tropes; I'm pretty sure that I could tell you what the broad themes were, but I doubt that I'd be able to connect any particular thematic dot to any particular brand. I know that all of the big wireless providers are currently offering various sorts of promotions, but I'd never be able to tell you which provider was offering which promotion. I know that the different cable companies are pushing different forms of pay-per-view, but it would never occur to me to try to keep track of the specifics.

When the category becomes a blur, we usually retain some general sense of what is happening within that category—a general set of associations, along with a general awareness of the latest competitive maneuverings—but we are hard-pressed to connect specifics to individual brands. We no longer see the trees for the forest.

And once this occurs, our relationship to the category becomes as revealing as our relationship to any of the brands therein. This is the second thing that happens when a category reaches hyper-maturity: Consumption becomes a window into how we feel about a category per se, irrespective of the intramural jockeyings of the brands within. Forget the distinctions between Miller, Coors, and Budweiser; it is enough to know that we think beer is a beverage for football-loving meatheads. Or that lingerie is "sexy and indulgent." Or that insurance is "necessary but boring." Or that car dealerships are "not to be trusted."

As an example, take a look at the following post:

> About Me: I couldn't live without chocolate.
> Also, I love drinking tea—I can't stand coffee.
> I'm a big believer in public transportation. I
> don't own a car and I hate SUVs!! I love body
> lotions, but I refuse to use anything animal-
> tested. And I never EVER wear perfume (yuk).

In this post, it is the category affiliations that matter, not the brand affiliations. SUVs versus public transportation. Tea versus coffee. Body lotion versus perfume. Brand references would be almost superfluous here; the mere record of category affiliations tells us everything we need to know.

Because businesspeople are understandably focused on their own brands, they tend to overlook how deep-seated and influential these category-level relationships can be. However, if you were to take the train from Boston to New York City you'd likely meet dozens of people who have eschewed air travel altogether. This is a category-level rejection; these are folks who are antagonistic toward the airline industry as a collective. Conversely, if you were to visit a cosmetics retailer like Sephora you'd likely meet dozens of self-professed makeup junkies. This is a category-level embrace; these are folks who are enamored with the category as a whole.

When we're intrigued by a category we'll be curious about the brands within it; when we're bored by a category we'll pay almost no attention at all. When we're enamored with a category we are eager to explore the options within it; when we're cynical about a category we look for the cheapest or most convenient thing. In all of these cases, our posture toward the category tends to dictate our behavior toward the brands it contains.

Not surprisingly, you can tell a lot about a person based on their consumption posture vis-à-vis particular categories. My best friend is a brand-sampling connoisseur when it comes to premium shampoos, an easy-to-please pragmatist when it comes to chocolate, and an utter indifferent when it comes to cars. My husband is a brand-collecting enthusiast when it comes to sneakers and guitars, a utilitarian when it comes to technology, and a cynic when it comes to golf clubs.

Predictable people are ones with predictable category postures: Most teenage girls love music, makeup, clothing, and fashion magazines. Unconventional people are ones with unconventional category postures: I know a seventeen-year-old girl who collects Tolkien memorabilia, hates makeup, and refuses to think about clothing.

In each of these depictions, allusions to category generalities communicate enough of the story to render the brand-specific details irrelevant. Meanwhile, notice how an individual's personal consumption medley still amounts to a kind of personality mosaic, more anthropological and culturally bound than a traditional personality test perhaps, but interpretive in a different, more iconographic sort of way.

In the late 1950s and early 1960s, a group of scholars led by Everett Rogers at Iowa State University introduced a theory of technology adoption (a theory known as the Diffusion of Innovations, later popularized in Geoffrey Moore's *Crossing the Chasm*) that proposed that there are some folks who are more naturally inclined to embrace unfamiliar products coming out of immature markets than others, and that it's possible to segment the potential market for a new product introduction according to this inclination. The theory caught, and the segmentation scheme—which included innovators, early adopters, early majority, late majority, and laggards—ended up becoming a core part of our business vernacular, particularly for entrepreneurial firms operating in newly emergent industries.

In recent years, it's occurred to me that it would be a revealing exercise to construct an alternative segmentation scheme designed to capture the other side of the coin: the ways in which people are inclined to respond to the overwhelming profusion of options emanating out of hyper-*mature* categories, categories with which they already have deep experience. Note that in these categories, the problem isn't one of lack of familiarity or fear of innovation; rather, it is one of product fatigue and cynicism.

If I were to play this exercise out, here is how I'd go about it.

• I'd start with the segment of folks I introduced to you earlier in this book: category *connoisseurs*. Connoisseurs have tremendous affection for the category and are discriminating with respect to their choices, but this doesn't necessarily lead to a particular brand preference. They are selective, informed, and picky, but they are variety seekers and brand samplers, too. Their loyalty is directed toward the category as opposed to any particular brand within it.

• The second segment would be people I'd describe as *savvy opportunists*. Opportunists are akin to connoisseurs in one respect: they are brand-agnostic category experts. The difference is that when they participate in the category, they do so without joy. Opportunists are transaction-oriented consumers whose posture toward the category could almost be described as competitive—they are coupon clippers, bargain hunters, rewards points accumulators. They're often cynical and disillusioned by what has happened in the category, but they maintain their comparative diligence for utilitarian reasons.

• The third segment would consist of folks I'd label *pragmatics*. Pragmatics are non-differentiators; they no longer expend the energy to keep abreast of the latest competitive permutations in the market.

They've grown skeptical of the differences between brand alternatives, so they make their buying decisions based on some combination of habit, routine, price, and convenience. An extreme version of a pragmatic would be an *indifferent,* someone who treats the category as almost pure commodity. (A psychologist would use the term "choice demotivation" to refer to this particular coping mechanism; it simply means that the more choice overload these folks experience, the less they care about which one they choose.)

• The fourth segment would consist of the *reluctants.* Reluctants are exactly that—reluctant consumers in the category. They dread participating in the market and would actually prefer to remain permanent category outsiders except for the fact that they occasionally have no choice. Their distaste, discomfort, and lack of familiarity with the category manifests as confusion, frustration, and awkwardness, and they're eager to exit the market as quickly as possible.

• The final segment would consist of the *brand loyalists.* These are the folks who, despite the number of competitive alternatives in the market, still exhibit a stubborn passion for a particular brand. They insist on sticking with their HP computers; they insist on sticking with their Häagen-Dazs. Their brand loyalty can appear somewhat quirky and retro to mainstream consumers given the hyper-maturity of the market; nonetheless, in most markets a lingering few of these hard-core loyalists manage to survive.

Certainly, all of these segments would have to accommodate some gradations: some pragmatists are more disaffected than others, while some cynics are more cynical than others. But my guess is that these five segments—connoisseurs, opportunists, pragmatics/indifferents, reluctants, and loyalists—would probably do a pretty good job of covering the bases, encompassing most of the ways that people cope with hypermature markets.

Moreover, what would be most interesting (and perhaps even most useful) about this segmentation scheme is what it would reveal about the categories to which it was applied. Consider, for example, the number of categories that would appear to have an unhealthy representation of savvy opportunists and reluctants. The airline industry seems to abound with such consumers, on the one hand catering to an army of disillusioned road warriors who have become expert at gaming the pricing system to maximize their frequent-flier miles using minimal dollars, while on the other hand catering to an army of reluctant leisure travelers who spend much of their trip reminding themselves how much they hate to travel by air.

Or consider the number of categories that appear to be dominated by some combination of opportunists and pragmatics. The cellular industry comes to mind here. Consumers in this industry seem to be either extremely savvy in their consumption decisions or not; regardless, there is an observable lack of affection in their attitude toward their carriers.

Or consider the number of categories in which the proportion of pragmatics appears to be growing with each passing year. A wide swath of categories comes to mind here—including some that occupy entire aisles in the drugstore. These are hyper-mature categories in which citizens have begun to question the credence of the advertised distinctions between brands and are thus inclined to adopt a "don't know, don't care" attitude.

Even more revealing would be to take some comparative snapshots of what these categories looked like ten years ago versus today, in terms of the anatomy of their customer bases. If one were to do this, my guess is that these snapshots would reveal a perceptible trend in category after category—the proportion of brand loyalists shrinking in conjunction with the growth of the various brand-agnostic segments in the market.

—⚬⚬⚬—

As I said earlier, there aren't too many things that I feel certain about when it comes to business, but one of them is that brand loyalty is becoming harder to come by. The irony is that the role of consumption in our lives—as an identity badge, as a form of cultural argot—has never been more prominent.

My sister-in-law, for example, could be characterized as a brand marketer's ideal target customer. Why?

Because she is someone for whom consumption has deep significance. Whether the product is T-shirts or shoes or hair products or baseball tickets or cocktails, consumption is one of the processes on which she relies to create texture, color, and flourish in her everyday life. And so she thinks about her consumption in a manner that is discriminating, self-aware, impassioned, and engaged.

And yet take a look at how this plays out:

- She is a connoisseur when it comes to spa products, vodka martinis, sandals, restaurants, and countless other products and services.

- She is a savvy opportunist when it comes to concert tickets, home furnishings, airline tickets, and a number of other products and services.

- She is a pragmatic when it comes to laptops, hotel reservations, car rentals, and so on.

- She is a reluctant when it comes to fast food, cable television service, and soda pop.

- And she is a brand loyalist only when it comes to accessories (Paul Frank), makeup (Princess Borghese), watches (ToyWatch), and a few fashion brands.

In other words, despite her considerable consumption energies, my sister-in-law possesses a surprisingly limited set of brand loyalties. In category after category, her consumption behaviors are saturated with the two essential ingredients for brand loyalty—passion and comparative expertise—and yet in category after category, these two ingredients have become disconnected from any such thing. It's almost as if she has the stuff to be a brand loyalist, but given the state of the markets in which she participates, she's simply come to know better.

My sister-in-law is not an exception in this regard. I can think of literally dozens of acquaintances in my social circle who consume with a similar degree of brio and yet reserve their loyalties for an equally paltry number of brands; my guess is that you can, too. When brand fidelity becomes this elusive despite the existence of hordes of savvy, passionate consumers such as these, it's hard not to get the sense that something is amiss.

escaping
the herd

SO here is the story to date. In the previous chapters, I have tried to make the argument that as a category matures, the companies within that category become increasingly apt to exhibit herdlike behaviors. I've also argued that the direction in which these companies tend to herd is fairly predictable, involving a kind of augmentation that is both monotonous and unrelenting in nature. The result is a category characterized by what I have referred to as heterogeneous homogeneity: There is an explosion of choices, but those choices are marked by differences that are meaningless to many of us.

Meanwhile, the product marketers who work in these companies have become masters at the dual arts of repetitive augmentation and competitive cloning. They have become gifted at accentuating non-essential distinctions; they have become skilled at cloaking sameness as differentiation. And they have become so immersed in the nuances of these crafts that they don't seem to realize the extent to which their claims have begun to lack face validity; they are too busy experiencing the category from the inside out. When I visited the folks at VOSS, it was a bit of a shock to discover that they earnestly believe their water tastes better than that of their competitors.

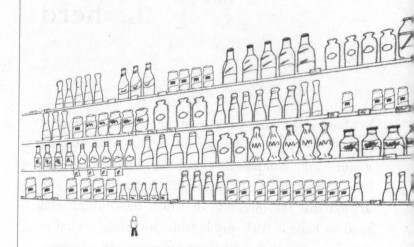

As for consumers, they experience the sequence of category evolution from the outside in. Over time they start to lose the trees for the forest, which means that their consumption patterns are increasingly driven by their relationship to the category writ large. This relationship may manifest in various forms, ranging from cynical opportunism to pragmatism to outright indifference; what it rarely does is manifest as brand loyalty.

It is this latter dynamic that most of us tend to experience at the most atomic level. I remember shopping for a television about a year ago and being overtaken by a sense of unease as I stared at the dozens of virtually identical flat-panel LCDs arrayed along the wall in the store. It was in that space that I felt my life-long loyalty to the Sony brand (a loyalty, it should be noted, that had been passed down from my parents when I was a child) begin to slip away. At first I tried to hold on to my loyalty by explaining my brand preference to the salesperson assisting me, but it wasn't long before I found myself allowing the salesperson (a category connoisseur, no surprise) to gently dissuade me from being so naive as to base my purchase on brand alone. By the end of my shopping excursion I had in fact settled on a more pragmatic purchase, and in that very moment became just another consumer in just another category, crossing that invisible line from brand loyalist to brand agnostic.

Today, moments like this are happening with banal regularity in one category after another, and because they are happening with such recurrence, their cumulative effect cannot be overstated. It is a critical inflection point in the life cycle of a category—when not only does brand loyalty start to wane, but the notion of brand loyalty itself starts to feel like a quaint anachronism. I remember almost blushing while trying to explain to the salesperson why I liked Sony televisions, particularly as I realized how undifferentiated the brand had become in the context of the category. When brand loyalty becomes this tough to defend, it is only a matter of time before it becomes fragile to the point of breakage.

One of the more popular sitcoms of the 1970s was a show called *Happy Days*. During the ten years of its run, it traced a familiar arc: It started off strong, got stronger over the next few years, and then peaked before succumbing to its inevitable decline. According to television lore, the show's final death knell came during an episode in which Fonzie found himself in the ludicrous position of having to water-ski over a shark; this was apparently the point at which even the show's most ardent followers began fleeing in droves. Since then, the phrase "jump the shark" has become an industry colloquialism, representing the juncture at which it is no longer possible to deny that the tide has shifted for a particular show, leaving little for even diehard loyalists to hang on to anymore.

In business, I believe a similar arc can be traced in product category after product category: As these categories mature, the products within them get progressively better over time, with consumers benefiting along the way. But somewhere along the line these categories jump the shark, having undergone too many plot twists and turns for consumers to stomach anymore. I felt the tide shift for me the last time I bought a television; over the past few years, I've experienced the shift in a couple of other categories as well. You may have, too, and if you have, you and I are both part of a consumption trend that I contend is one of the most significant challenges facing business today.

———

In the next section of the book, however, I'd like to offer an amendment to the above argument. Because what I actually believe is that most categories tend to evolve in a predictable fashion *until*. Until what? Until a company comes along and does something unpredictable, something anomalous . . . that ends up stirring both the competition and consumers out of their normal routines. And as a consequence, that company is able to steer the trajectory of the category in an unexpected direction.

The brands that make me sit up and pay attention are exactly these: Brands that are able to entice people out of their entrenched consumption patterns. Brands that are able to make pragmatics and indifferents want to go the extra mile to buy *their* brand. Brands that are able to turn reluctants into enthusiasts, opportunists into loyalists.

This is not an easy thing to accomplish. As I noted earlier, the attitudes we bring to a category tend to reflect deeply embedded category stereotypes that have been reinforced by brand after brand, year after year. This is why it's difficult for us to imagine any amount of marketing persuasion that would ever make us look forward to, say, traveling on an airplane or signing up for a new cell phone contract. The truth is, most cell phone carriers *do* make you feel like a hostage. Airline travel *has* become a demeaning cattle call. All bottled water *is* the same. Once we develop a particular set of category stereotypes, they tend to become as ingrained as a natural born reflex. And yet some brands manage to do exactly that—they are able to turn our stereotypes on their heads, earning our affection and our respect along the way.

When I was in college many years ago, I remember there being quite a bit of buzz about a young comedian who was performing at Broadway's Lyceum Theatre. If

I told you that the comedian was Whoopi Goldberg it would almost ruin the story because the Whoopi of today is a well-known, outspoken Oscar-winning actress with a sometimes clownish public persona. But back in the day, Whoopi was just a nobody with a one-woman comedy act. I remember going to the show with a set of expectations—I expected it to be funny, perhaps even side-splittingly funny—but as it turned out, the most memorable aspect of the show was not its humor but its poignancy; the show was streetwise and gritty, at times heartbreakingly so. What Whoopi showed up with that night was a trenchant mixture of performance art and cultural observation and, yes, a bit of comedy, too, but whatever laughter she generated was almost beside the point. I should add that the performance was a tour de force.

When most businesses think about managing our expectations, they tend to think of those expectations as running along a vertical axis, which means that they can either exceed our expectations by delighting us (a good thing), or they can fail to meet those expectations by disappointing us (a bad thing). What they forget is that there is another axis that runs orthogonal to the vertical one—it is the axis that comes into play when a business offers us something that fails to meet our expectations but resounds in an entirely unanticipated way. Whoopi's performance may not have made me laugh out loud, but it created resonance of an entirely different sort.

Along the same lines, I was watching an old Tom and Jerry cartoon the other day with my kids and was struck by how mesmerizing it is to watch a piece of Swiss cheese turn into a flying carpet, or a diamond ring turn into a hula hoop before turning into a circus trapeze. Cartoons delight us not by exceeding our expectations but by invalidating them. They ignore the laws of nature and because they do, they don't compete against live action, they offer an alternative reality to it.

These are the brands that I'm inclined to pay the most attention to: the ones that treat our expectations as nothing more than straw men. They recognize that the challenge is to render our expectations irrelevant in the context of what else they are offering, and so they take it upon themselves to offer us an alternative reality to our established one.

What's interesting is that this doesn't mean that these brands are necessarily "better" or "worse" than other offerings in the market. It does, however, mean that they are *differentiated*—differentiated in a way that allows them to cultivate a different relationship with their customers, differentiated in a way that allows them to stand apart from the herd. They thus serve as exemplars of the thesis I've offered from the start—that the way to think about differentiation is not as the offspring of competition, but as escape from competition altogether.

———

Some of the brands that I'll be discussing in the following chapters are big brands with which I'm sure you're familiar. Others are smaller brands of which you may never have heard. What they all have in common is that they are what I like to call "idea brands." Instead of emerging out of anything as tangible as traditional market research, these brands emerged from something much less certain—the insight that it is possible to do things in an exceedingly distinct way.

If you've ever been in the market for a new house, you know that one of the biggest decisions a home buyer frequently has to make is whether to buy a house and renovate it, or whether to buy a house and do a complete teardown. To buy and renovate is to tinker with the superficial while keeping the foundation and the basic layout of the house intact. But to attempt a complete teardown is a profoundly different animal; it requires starting from scratch with nothing but an empty lot. This can be an unnerving thing, because it involves contending with countless degrees of freedom. It can also be a liberating thing for precisely the same reason.

The idea brands that I'm going to introduce you to represent the teardown approach; they offer a whole-scale rethinking of the value proposition in their respective categories. What this means is that they owe their existence to no insignificant amount of conceptual inspiration. Someone, somewhere, had to actually sit down and imagine what a radically different sort of house might look like.

It's disheartening to consider how diminished the role of conceptual inspiration has become in hyper-mature categories, in which companies have become so consumed with keeping pace with the competition that they often lack the bandwidth to even *try* to generate inspiration. Which is another reason why I'm attracted to the idea brands I'm about to introduce you to—because they contain a hint of what I believe is becoming more uncommon than ever. At some point in their histories, the people behind these brands put in the creative work required to produce a conceptual breakthrough, competition be damned. And because they were able to successfully execute on their inspirations, they were able to produce an outcome that was nothing less than category transforming.

—◦—

Given the competitiveness of the markets in which most businesses operate today, it's harder than ever to be an outlier. It's harder than ever to sustain a lopsided value proposition. It's harder than ever to risk a positioning strategy that places your brand several standard deviations away from the mean. I completely recognize this.

It's harder still to come up with a market-disrupting strategy that generates positive returns for both customers and shareholders. Again, I recognize this. And yet while the term "disruption" typically suggests a destruction or violation of what exists, the idea brands that I'll be introducing you to have somehow managed to produce a creative destructive; they have somehow managed to become rebels *with* a cause.

What this means is that these are brands that are creating even as they are destroying. They are constructing even as they are disrupting. And in the process, they are attempting to bring to life a counter-factual, which, if you think about it, is either crazy or quixotic or both. On the other hand, this is why I believe these brands are deserving of study: Because they are, at the very least, trying to play the story forward in a different way. They are trying to envision the market through the lens of alternative future possibility.

Of course, the problem with pointing to certain brands as positive examples of anything is that there is an obvious selection bias. Great brands are experiential and personal, which means that the only legitimate arbiter of whether a brand is great is anyone who happens to experience it. Put another way, I'm no more an expert on what makes a brand praiseworthy than you are, and it would be hubris for me to presume otherwise.

But keep in mind my objective here. My intention is to start a conversation—not only about what it means to differentiate in this day and age, but about what it means to offer a group of jaded, cynical, bored citizens something that they will in some way regard as special. The brands that I've chosen to highlight share nothing more than the fact that they have given me pause. I don't necessarily "like" all of them and I certainly wouldn't purchase all of them for myself, but I see how they have managed to strike a chord with some segment of the market and this intrigues me. And so I offer them to you as a conversation starter.

I've tried to lump these brands together using a set of chapter divisions and labels, but even this lumping is loose and arbitrary. The labels I've used and the categorizations I've adopted are by no means authoritative and by no means correct; they are merely the mechanism via which I hope to begin deconstructing how these companies have managed to create separation from their competition.

As a final note, it should be evident by now that there is no question in my mind that there are big chunks of the business core that are simply broken. The most obvious manifestation of this is what I have described as a monolithic competitive herd. The silver lining in this is that there is now a window of opportunity for outliers to emerge; after all, in order for there to be a rebel, there must first be an establishment against which to rebel. And so, much as cartoons derive their power from their contrast to live action, what I hope you'll see is that idea brands derive their power from the very thing they are attempting to subvert. In some strange respects, then, the companies that I am about to present to you can be thought of this way—as palliatives that owe their existence to the disease.

part 2

no contest

(celebration)

reversal

the adoption of a new technology can make for an illuminating historical bookmark. In 1995, I was a grad student in California and unbeknownst to me, my world was about to change. It started innocently enough; I had just purchased a new laptop and a friend of mine told me I needed to download a program called Netscape and use it to get on the internet. "Start by typing in Yahoo!" she told me.

Back then we still used awkward terms like "cyberspace," "the infobahn," and "the information superhighway" to refer to the web, and the only way most people knew to get onboard was by using Yahoo! or one of the other portals—AOL, Excite, AltaVista. The funny thing was, none of us were exactly clear on what we were supposed to be *doing* online; all we knew was that there were swirling currents of information out there and if you wanted to tap into them, you needed a guide, a virtual shepherd if you will. This is what the search portals provided; they promised to hold our hands as we ventured into this unregulated ocean of content.

For me, everything began and ended with Yahoo! When I first began using the service, the company was a baby really, only a couple of years old and just beginning to find its way in the world. But as my online experience grew, the baby grew, too. Or maybe it was the other way around—as Yahoo! grew, my online experience expanded as a consequence.

First, Yahoo! added news headlines to its homepage. Then stock quotes and the latest sports scores. Then weather. Personals. Email. Auctions. And with each new addition to its homepage, a new piece of the internet opened up to me. Games. Online classifieds. A calendar service. Travel information. Every day, a new feature, a new benefit to explore. Job listings. Horoscopes. Entertainment news. This was augmentation-by-addition at the rate of hyperspeed, and because all of the major search portals—Excite, AltaVista, AOL—were caught in the wave, within a few years all of them had evolved into online smorgasbords offering a swollen buffet of information and services:

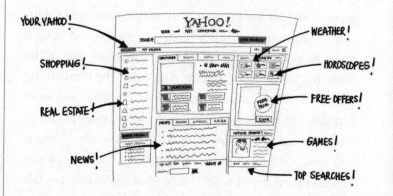

These companies were not just setting the competitive pace for the industry, they were setting the consumption standard for how people accessed information on the web. And if ever there was a time when it would've

seemed easy to be a prognosticator—that is, easy to predict what the Portal of the Future would look like—this
reckoned to be the time, because the evolutionary trajectory of the category couldn't have appeared more clear. It
seemed patently obvious that we were headed for a future
in which all of the major portals would offer endless front
pages filled with even more benefits and more services.
The Portal of Tomorrow would be bigger, better, busier,
noisier, and flashier than the Portal of Today, just as the
Portal of Today was bigger, better, busier, noisier, and
flashier than the Portal of Yesterday.

But then something happened to call that future
into question. And that something was Google.

Google has become such a routinized part of our
daily regimen that it's easy to forget how stunning it was
in its earliest incarnation. Stunning, not for what it did,
but for what it didn't do. As a late entry into the portal
game, Google's homepage wasn't just simple, it was
stripped-down, it was naked, it was a downright *vacuum*
of information. Whereas Yahoo! offered an ocean,
Google offered a blank slate. Its homepage consisted of
a single element: a text-entry box with a search button.

And what most ordinary users didn't realize at the time was how preordained this was. From its inception, the company had made a conscious commitment to delivering the cleanest homepage possible, even if it meant withholding benefits that consumers had come to expect from online portals. There was not a single visible sign that Google offered news. Or weather. Or stock information. Or shopping. There were no pictures, no fancy graphics, no nothing. In other words, just as its primary competitors—Yahoo! AOL, and the like—were preparing to shift things into fifth gear, Google stepped in and threw things into reverse.

Google is what I like to refer to as a "reverse-positioned brand." A reverse-positioned brand is a very particular kind of idea brand, one that makes the deliberate decision to defy the augmentation trend in a category in which customers have come to expect augmentation. What this means is that there is a commitment to withholding benefits that the rest of the industry considers necessary to compete. Reverse brands say no where others say yes. And they do so openly. Without apology.

Consider the implications of this for a minute. In business generally and in marketing specifically, there are few greater sins than failing to meet customer expectations. So nothing is likely to raise eyebrows more quickly than a decision to strip away benefits that consumers expect to receive. This is why the concept of reversal goes against every instinct a businessperson has. When the entire category is racing north, it is no trivial matter to point yourself due south.

But that's not all. Most stripped-down brands tend to be the market dregs. You know the type—bare-bones discounters that garner scant respect from their high-end brethren. Brands like Motel 6. Kmart. Bob's Discount Furniture. Family Dollar Stores.

But reverse-positioned brands avoid this fate by doing a second thing that is equally audacious. They take their stripped-down value proposition and infuse it with some unexpected form of extravagance. That is, they surround their otherwise parsimonious product with their own version of splendor, and it is this inspired bundle of attributes that leads to the firm's unique positioning in the category.

—

Here is an example. If you were to have examined a snapshot of the airline industry about a decade ago, you would've seen an industry full of fliers who had grown accustomed to receiving a particular set of benefits from the major carriers, including free meals on every flight, the option of flying in first or business class, and a full range of pricing options, such as round-trip fares that were cheaper than one-way fares.

In 2000, however, JetBlue came along and brashly took these benefits away from us. Gone was the free meal service. Gone was the option of a first- or business-class seat. Gone were the round-trip discounts (all of JetBlue's fares were based on one-way travel).

At the same time, JetBlue infused its otherwise elemental value proposition with a kind of exorbitance that most of us had never before associated with a budget carrier. Plush leather seats that extended all the way to the rear of the plane. A personal entertainment and satellite television system located in every seat. A guaranteed promise to never bump a passenger.

This is what reverse brands do: They take away what we expect, but then give us what we don't. They say no where others say yes, but they also say yes where others say no. The result is a value proposition that feels almost "inside-out" to us.

Google, too, gifted us with splashes of indulgence. Perhaps the most generous aspect of Google's homepage was the utter absence of advertising. Before Google came along, the unspoken agreement in the industry was that the trade-off for free online services was an advertising-heavy environment. Companies took this trade-off for granted, and users did, too.

Given this, there was something almost decadent about the purity of the Google experience. To open up the Google homepage was like walking into one of those ultra-luxe boutiques where a minimum of merchandise is presented in the most pristine retail setting. There can be elegance in restraint, and Google seemed to understand this, offering up a kind of quiet taste that was nowhere else to be found online.

Google's homepage displayed other touches of subtle extravagance as well, almost as an aside: lightning-fast search results (so fast that the site would actually reveal the number of milliseconds consumed by the search) and a whimsical logo that mutated in celebration of certain calendar occasions. Together, these benefits added up to a value proposition that didn't drown us in a plethora of benefits, but instead suggested quality of a more discerning sort.

Again, this is what reverse brands do: They eliminate, but they also elevate. They strip things down, even as they sweeten things up. The result is a fusion of the basic with the sublime, a fusion that may seem strange, unfamiliar, or even disconcerting at first encounter—but is nothing if not distinctive.

The truth is, back in the late nineties, Yahoo! AOL, and the other portals might have claimed to be different from each other, but their value propositions were essentially the same. The same goes for Delta, American, and United; they might have claimed to be different from each other, but their value propositions were essentially the same. Google and JetBlue entered their respective markets with an uncommon blend of unlikely elements. So while their competitors remained clustered and herdlike, these two brands managed to stand apart.

———

In business, it is easy to fall into the habit of thinking that the way to be better is to simply do more. It is easy to think that the way to improve your laundry detergent is to simply strengthen your fabric softener, or to offer a few additional fragrances. It is easy to think that the way to improve your airline is to simply add a few benefits to your frequent-flier program, or to throw in some new pricing options.

In some respects, this reflexive impulse could even be regarded as commendable. More often than not, whenever you see a company that is constantly tweaking its value proposition with improvement upon improvement, you are looking at a business that is dedicated to being the absolute best that it can be. The Ritz-Carlton. Nordstrom. The Four Seasons. These are businesses that care about their customers, and because they care about their customers, they take pride in operating under the assumption that no matter how good a job they're doing, there are still likely to be customers out there who aren't 100 percent satisfied. This assumption then serves as a motivator to deliver better service, better products, better quality.

However, if the story of augmentation has a parable, it is that it's possible to improve yourself all the way to mediocrity. We saw this in a previous chapter. When every restaurant in town is offering a fabulous all-you-can-eat buffet, it's only a matter of time before we cease to be impressed by any of them.

This is why the notion of reversal runs so counter to conventional business intuition. A reverse-positioned firm is one that refuses to get on the augmentation treadmill, not because it doesn't care about its customers, but because it is operating under an inverse assumption—that given the hyper-maturity of the category, there are probably lots of folks out there who are *over*-satisfied, i.e., who are being given an inflated set of benefits they don't necessarily care about. This assumption then serves as a motivator to streamline the value proposition, as opposed to further inflate it.

Of course, just because folks are over-satisfied doesn't mean that they're looking for a conventionally austere, low-end product, either. They may not want everything, but this doesn't mean they'd be happy with nothing. And so the reverse brand tries to concoct an unlikely brew, consisting of something less, but something more, too. It looks to create a symbiosis of elements that we've been trained to believe don't belong together. The idea is to be an oxymoron, and an agreeable one at that.

———

Here is another example. Imagine that you are newly married. And you are standing with your spouse in the middle of a specialty furniture store, say, an Ethan Allen or a Jordan's Furniture, trying to buy your first living room set. And because you are buying this living room set, you are not in the best of moods; as a matter of fact, you are the very picture of category reluctance. Nor are you alone in your ill temper; your spouse hasn't cracked a smile since you entered the store, and now that you think about it, the entire store appears to be filled with folks who look like they'd rather be somewhere else. Everybody, it seems, is a category reluctant.

In truth, you are experiencing what furniture industry mavens have known for years: People in this country loathe the process of furniture shopping. If you're anything like the typical American, you're likely to hang on to your sofa for much longer than your car and you're likely to change your spouse at least as often as your dining room table, about 1.5 times in your lifetime.

Now, to their credit, all of your local furniture

retailers are well aware of your displeasure, so they've gone to great lengths to make the experience as pleasant as possible for you. They've beefed up their product selections to give you an extraordinary amount of variety to choose from. They've filled their stores with sales consultants to assist you with the process of visualizing and designing your new living room. They've established delivery services to transport your purchases home for you. And most important, they know that you don't want to have to repeat the process again in the near future, so they've made sure that the furniture they are selling is built to last a lifetime—*"this is the last living room set you'll ever have to buy."*

But here's what's interesting. As you stand there in that furniture store, none of these service augmentations succeed in making a dent in your attitude. On the contrary, the augmentations themselves are their own turnoff. You find yourself irritated by the enormous product selection. You find yourself annoyed by the heavy-handed sales consultants. You resent the burden of having to choose a living room set that you know you're going to be stuck with for the rest of your life.

The self-defeating anti-logic of augmentation is that it can not only fail to increase satisfaction but actually diminish it. As a business, the surest indication that this is happening is when customers start turning your positives into their negatives. You surround them with helpful sales reps and they resent the intrusiveness. You offer them a homepage filled with news, weather, sports, and information, and they complain about the clutter and slow load times. You offer them free meals on their flights and they tell you they taste like crap. It's a classic case of the cure devolving into the disease.

——

That said, one of the most popular business cases I've ever written tells the story of IKEA North America. My guess is that you're familiar with the brand; according to the agencies that measure these things, it's among the most powerful consumer brands in the world.

Most global brands build their reputations around a set of positives—the good things they do for their customers. What's intriguing about IKEA is that it has consciously built its reputation around a set of negatives—the service elements it has deliberately chosen to withhold from its customers. Pull a random individual off the street and ask them if they've ever heard of IKEA, and chances are they'll say something like "Isn't that the furniture store that makes you do your own delivery and assembly . . . ?" This is a company that has, from the start, taken as much pride in what it doesn't do as what it does.

Indeed, when IKEA launched in the United States, it did so with a value proposition that was almost absurd in its economy, particularly when viewed against the cushiony offerings of the other specialty furniture retailers in the market. It offered minimal variety: Its furniture came in just four basic styles—Scandinavian, modern, country, and young Swede. It offered a dearth of shopping assistance: Its stores were expressly designed to propel customers through the cavernous spaces without the aid of sales consultants. It offered no delivery, no assembly: Buyers were expected not only to transport their purchases home on their own but to assemble them as well. It didn't even offer the promise of durability; rather, the company openly conceded that its furniture was unlikely to last forever and encouraged buyers to think of their products as soft goods that would need to be replaced in a few years.

And yet IKEA wrapped its offering in a dazzling set of attributes that belied its bare-bones image. IKEA shoppers could drop their children off at a brightly designed, company-operated day care center while they shopped. They could stop for lunch at a café that served delicacies like smoked salmon, lingonberry tarts, and Swedish meatballs. They could purchase items besides furniture—colorful housewares and cleverly designed toys not available at other retailers. In short, IKEA shunned the gloomy, warehouselike atmosphere associated with most discount furniture retailers in favor of a cheerful, airy, ultra-modern look and feel. This Euro-flavored "retailtainment" environment was combined with a product selection that, despite the limited number of choices, conveyed a particular Scandinavian style—one that communicated symmetry, simplicity, and a lack of pretentiousness all at once.

This is what makes IKEA a reverse brand: It gives us something less, but it gives us something more, too. It smoothly combines elements that we aren't accustomed to seeing together. It is an oxymoronic brand, yes, but one that's uncommonly suited for the oxymoronic consumer—the hard-to-please, over-satisfied sort.

In fact, if I had to identify the secret of IKEA's appeal, here's what I'd say: IKEA is a brand that has discovered the cool of unapologetic contradiction. It is stingy; it is indulgent. It says yes; it says no. It strips things down; it sweetens things up. It has stumbled upon a dialectic, and it has somehow figured out how to make that dialectic sing.

—————

The concept of over-satisfaction only makes sense in a world in which we have too much. As I like to tell my students, jaded is the new stoned. We are living in a culture in which the hallmark of sophisticated consumption is a refusal to be impressed for very long.

What makes this scary for a business is that it means you can offer all the augmentation in the world—the fanciest all-you-can-eat buffets, the armies of sales assistants, the jam-packed homepages—and it won't necessarily buy you much, at least for very long. Satiation has the perverse effect of making nothing taste good anymore.

And yet there is a strange corollary to this, a corollary that goes something like this: In a saturated world, there can be a fresh appreciation for the elimination of benefits, as long as that elimination is thoughtfully executed. When people are accustomed to having too much, they will luxuriate in the absence of things they've come to take for granted.

The fact of the matter is, a trip to IKEA can be a colossal hassle. Not only does it typically require an hour or two of driving to get there (there are only a few dozen stores sprinkled across the country), but the selection, loading, and hauling process can easily consume an entire day. There is also the monumental assembly challenge that awaits you after you unpack your goods. And God forbid you actually want to transport the furniture a year or two after you've assembled it; the stuff is sufficiently unsturdy to raise serious doubts as to whether it could survive any such relocation.

And yet here is what I find fascinating about the IKEA phenomenon: When you listen to IKEA lovers defend the brand (and believe me, there are lots of them out there), they won't just rave about the positives, they'll rationalize the negatives, too. They'll admit that a trip to IKEA can be inconvenient, but they'll try to persuade you that it's "an expedition, an adventure." They'll concede that the shopping task can take a while to complete, but they'll claim that the time in the store feels "like being in Disneyland." They'll agree that the assembly process can be tedious, but they'll argue that it's also "empowering." And they'll smile when you question them about the furniture's flimsiness, noting that it can be "liberating" to not have to make a long-term commitment to their purchases.

What you're hearing here is rare brand alchemy—the sound of customers turning a brand's negatives into their own personal positives. IKEA has somehow managed to pull off an inversion of the spoiled-customer hypothesis. Its customers toil and suffer, yet they feel incredibly well cared for nonetheless.

From the perspective of a businessperson, it would be convenient if the relationship between customer pampering and customer satisfaction were a perfectly linear one, but the story of IKEA underscores how much fuzzier the reality can be. There can be satisfaction in pampering, sure, but there can be satisfaction in deprivation, too, as long as that deprivation is offered in a manner that is meaningful to people. Exclusive spas play off this psychology on a regular basis; they deprive and indulge, at the same time.

This is why reverse brands are so reflective of the contemporary culture in which they reside. Because implicit in their positioning is the neo-understanding that in an over-augmented world, a lack of trimmings can have a certain self-righteous appeal. And so they offer us a bit of deprivation, sprinkled with an unexpected splash of indulgence—just the thing to bring our taste buds back to life.

In California, there is a reverse-positioned burger chain called In-N-Out Burger. Unlike its fast-food competitors, In-N-Out Burger has no Happy Meal clones, no children's menu, no salads, no desserts; instead, it offers a mere six items on a menu that hasn't changed in decades. However, there is a lot going on beneath the surface: every item on the menu is made from scratch, using fresh (not frozen) ingredients, and customers "in the know" can request items off an un-advertised "secret menu" that can only be learned about through word of mouth. What kind of restaurant offers food alternatives that it doesn't tell everyone about? In-N-Out Burger does, and in a category filled with pragmatics and known for its closet consumption, its customers are outspoken fanatics.

It's difficult to overstate this. When the first In-N-Out Burger in Utah opened a few years ago, a local reporter stopped in to see what all the fuss was about and found among the crowd a group of students from Brigham Young University who had driven more than five hundred miles for their lunch. In 2006, celebutante Paris Hilton was handcuffed blocks away from an In-N-Out for allegedly drunk driving; she admitted later on air to Ryan Seacrest that "I was really hungry, and I wanted to have an In-N-Out Burger." Customers routinely brag about the lengths to which they are willing to go—how far they are willing to drive, how long they are willing to wait in line—for an In-N-Out burger, and some have even been known to install "In-N-Out Finder" applications on their cell phones and PDAs.

In-N-Out Burger. IKEA. JetBlue. What all of these brands have in common is that they have been able to cultivate the most elusive of all customer segments: folks willing to be missionaries for their brand. Which is not to say that these reverse brands are for everyone; well-defined brands almost never are. It is simply to say that there is an astonishing amount of loyalty concentrated around these brands in spite of the fact that they all compete in industries in which loyalty is hard to come by.

When you remove benefits from a value proposition, you are in some sense crystallizing things. You are eliminating the extraneous in order to shed new light on the fundamental. Reverse brands can be startling in their clarity for precisely this reason.

And yet reverse brands can also be wonderfully difficult to pigeonhole. They aren't your typical high-end brands; they are far too streamlined for that. They aren't your typical low-end brands; they are too well appointed for that. Instead, they reject any manner of typecast, which only goes to show that in categories overwhelmed by sameness, this kind of outlier status can be quite the magnet.

We have a tendency to assume that history advances through a series of cumulative steps, that progress is synonymous with forward motion. But reverse brands serve as a reminder that this isn't always the case; history can advance through a series of progressive reversals as well. The television of the future may have more buttons, but it is equally possible that it will have fewer. The appliances of the future may be of the kind that last longer, but it is equally possible that they will be of the kind that are disposable.

If twenty years ago you had predicted that the only brand that would ever be able to cultivate enthusiastic loyalists in the furniture category would be the one that was in many ways the biggest hassle, I probably would've dismissed you as being crazy. If ten years ago you had predicted that the number one search portal on the internet would be the one flaunting the fewest number of benefits on its homepage, I probably would've thought you were nuts.

And yet today, both of these things are very much true. What this implies is that when it comes to our consumption preferences, what we want tomorrow is probably going to be informed by what we have too much of today. It is only when we are drowning in choices that we are going to feel liberated when someone takes them away. It's only when we're feeling suffocated by customer service that we're going to feel grateful for its absence. Less is more only when more has become a commodity.

That's why it is an irony that, on paper, the strategy of reversal is always going to look like the opposite of improvement. Anything that looks like a rejection of existing category trends is by definition going to look like a rejection of the advances the category has achieved in recent years, and more generally, a rejection of progress itself. However, what should be evident by now is that companies that embrace reversal are actually attempting to pull off something more enlightened than this. They are trying to beat a forward retreat; theirs is a reversal that is precocious for its foresight.

In the process, these brands manage to throw their competitive peers into the most uncomfortable position of all—that of an uncertain backpedal. In fact, if you watch their competitors closely, you can almost see the thought bubbles appearing above their heads—*Hmmm . . . maybe we need to start simplifying the fare structure on our flights, too . . . Maybe we need to begin thinking about streamlining our website. . . .* As a business, it's never any fun to be on the defensive, and yet this is exactly what happens—reverse brands put their peers on the defensive by forcing them to reevaluate the rationality of their own value propositions.

—⁓—

About ten years ago, a director by the name of Christopher Nolan released an ultra-noir psychological thriller called *Memento* about a guy suffering from short-term memory loss. What was remarkable about the film was that it unfolded backward in time, each scene stacked in reverse chronological order. And yet the movie itself was a series of revelations. Eye-opening, unanticipated revelations. I watched the movie again recently, and as I did, it occurred to me that this is what reverse brands do. They reveal, even as they reverse.

When Nintendo introduced the Wii in 2006, the video-game console wars were in full swing, and the release of each new generation of console would mark a new escalation in the arms race—with faster processors, beefier storage capacities, higher-resolution graphics. But Nintendo opted out of this race by giving us a console that was a lot less of the things we were expecting, and a lot more of the things we weren't. And the result was a revelation. An eye-opening, unanticipated revelation.

All it takes is a single firm to come along and alter the evolutionary trajectory of an entire category. All it takes is a single firm to come along and change our predictions of what the future is going to look like. Roll a marble on a flat surface and it will follow a straight and predictable path . . . until something comes along to create a tilt in the surface. Google did this ten years ago—it came along and created a tilt in the surface. IKEA came along and did the same, as did JetBlue and Nintendo Wii.

Maybe this is a better way to say it, then: Reverse brands create a kind of tilt in the surface—of progress, of evolution, of expectation. They draw us down a divergent path by applying pressure in exactly the place where we least anticipate it.

⸻

As a final observation, I should note that IKEA is a very lopsided brand. Google is a lopsided brand. In-N-Out Burger is a lopsided brand. And the problem with lopsided brands is that they are inherently imbalanced, which means that they are always under pressure to move toward a more well-rounded position. The IKEA of today is constantly fielding demands to offer delivery services, assembly services, and so on, and faces an ongoing struggle to figure out how to respond to these demands without diluting the purity of its value proposition. The Google of today has grown into a business of enormous complexity offering a full array of online products, and faces an ongoing struggle to figure out how to offer these products without impugning the cleanliness of its original brand promise. It remains to be seen whether these two brands, not to mention the other reverse brands mentioned in this chapter, are able to successfully negotiate these tensions going forward.

Still, I wouldn't count these brands out. Over the years, I've learned a lot from watching these brands operate, and one of the things I've discovered is that for no other reason than the fact that these companies originated from such a different starting point than their competitors, they've been able to enjoy years of stand-alone differentiation. And in a world of copycats, that is no small accomplishment.

breakaway

here's a question for you: If you could own your very own household robot, what would you have it do for you?

I tossed this question out to a bunch of my friends recently and the answers came back like this: "I'd have it do my vacuuming," one of them said. "I'd have it do my dishes," said another. "I'd have it mow the lawn." "I'd have it answer my email." "I'd have it clean my bathrooms."

What's fun about a question like this is that it requires no preface. A robot is something that all of us "get," so I don't have to explain what one is, I don't have to explain what one looks like. We've all managed to develop a shared archetype of the concept, to the point where if I asked you to draw a picture of one, your picture would almost certainly look a lot like mine.

Considering that none of us have actually encountered one of these androids in real life, this is a pretty curious thing. In the software community, the term "vaporware" refers to a software product that doesn't actually exist even though it's already been announced to the public. Robots are a kind of vaporware of the highest order; they don't actually exist yet (at least in

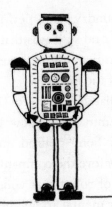

the form in which we imagine them), and yet in many ways, they've already been marketed to us—by filmmakers and science fiction writers, among others. The result is a product category (ROBOTS) that exists in our heads even if it doesn't yet exist in our homes.

I'll tell you what: If I owned a robot, I'd want it to be my household servant and personal assistant all in one. I'd want it to bring me dinner; I'd want it to clean my house. I'd want it to make my travel arrangements; I'd want it to pay my bills. I'd want it to have a voice with a lilting Singaporean accent and be fluent in multiple languages. I'd want it to have all these things, and a sense of humor to boot.

⸺

About a dozen years ago, a group of Sony engineers led by Toshitada Doi, one of the company's leading computer engineers, became intrigued by the prospect of building a personal household robot for the everyday consumer. Wouldn't it be fabulous, Doi wondered, if we could one day create a robot that would wash the dishes, do the laundry, and perform other chores around the house? And so it was that Doi and his team launched the preliminary development process for the household robot of the future.

Almost immediately, however, Doi found himself confronting a dilemma. He knew that regardless of how much money Sony poured into the project, it would take years before the company would be able to produce the kind of robot that consumers tended to associate with their mental archetype of a ROBOT. Current artificial intelligence (AI) technology was simply too primitive; current robotic engineering simply too crude. Whatever the team produced in the short term was bound to be buggy, unreliable, with limited functionality—a robot sure to disappoint, in other words.

Given this dilemma, Doi made a rather peculiar decision: He decided that the way to circumvent any potential consumer disappointment, at least in the near term, was to give the product a puppylike appearance and market it as a pet. Not as a robot per se, but as a robotic *pet*. Named AIBO. That looked something like this:

In addition, Doi decided that when it came to functionality, the product would be marketed as having no more utility than an actual puppy, which is to say, no practical utility at all. The AIBO was to be positioned instead as a *companion*. As AIBO's general manager, Takeshi Yazawa, put it, "In the end, we all agreed . . . AIBO loves you, you love AIBO, and that's it."

In fact, the entire marketing endeavor had an offbeat, fanciful flavor to it. Promotional materials referred to the AIBO as an autonomous pet with an individualistic personality—literally, a "mind of its own"—while the advertising copy was infused with a strong tongue-in-cheek inflection. As for the primary target market for the device, it consisted of senior citizens, parents with small children, and busy young professionals—people who wanted the "fun of a living creature, without the messy inconvenience."

The approach was particularly quirky when you considered the guts of the machine. The AIBO was no cheap plaything—it was priced at a whopping $2,500 (a price that didn't even cover the company's cost of production) and it included some pretty hard-core technology: the latest artificial intelligence, a 64-bit RISC processor, a 180,000-pixel color CCD camera with infrared sensors. And yet these engineering superlatives were downplayed relative to the overall message to the market. The word to consumers was that the AIBO was a pet—a playful, mischievous, and independent-minded pet—as close to the real thing as modern technology was capable of producing.

When my children were just a few years old, they went through a phase where all they did was categorize things: *An apple is a fruit. A horse is an animal. A flower is a plant.* Categorization was their way of making connections, of making sense of their world. So they'd play grouping games in preschool: *"One of these things just doesn't belong . . ."* They'd store their toy trains in one box, their miniature cars in another. And with each passing day, they'd grasp some new insight into the order of things: *Mommy, did you know that the sun is a star? That a dolphin is a mammal? That a Y is both a vowel and a consonant?*

Some ninety years ago, Walter Lippmann published *Public Opinion,* a classic piece of social commentary in which he wrote, "For the most part we do not first see and then define, we define first and then see." What Lippmann was essentially saying was that as humans our tendency to categorize is reflexive, automatic. We need to know what something *is* before we can figure out how we're supposed to relate to it. So we have categories for people: white-collar, blue-collar. For things: solids, liquids, gases. For colors: blue, red, green. And so on. And if it just so happens that we encounter something that we are unable to peg—say, a passerby with indeterminate gender—the ambiguity has the potential to stop us in our tracks: *Hey, was that a man or a woman?* It's like that old *Saturday Night Live* sketch featuring Julia Sweeney as the androgynous "Pat"; we have trouble moving forward until we get the basic definitions sorted out.

And yet here is the thing. When it comes to the physical sciences, our categorizations tend to be, for the most part, rigorous and objective; they reflect innate differences between solids and liquids, or between protons and neutrons. When it comes to the biological sciences, our categorizations are equally non-discretionary; they reflect intrinsic discrepancies between mammals and fish, or between DNA and RNA. But when it comes to our everyday artifacts—the routine *stuff* we consume on a daily basis—our categorizations are not even vaguely scientific; they are remarkably contrived, and flagrantly so.

The point is particularly relevant to the realm of business. Here, the answer to the question "What makes a thing a thing?" can be strikingly hollow. Cereal is cereal because it happens to be food broken down into spoon-sized bits; if the pieces were any larger, we'd have to call them cookies. A Frappuccino is a Frappuccino because it's sold at Starbucks and priced accordingly; sold anywhere else, it'd have to be considered a caffeinated milkshake. This is some pretty skin-deep stuff.

But even if at some subterranean level we are aware of this, we allow these distinctions to drive our behaviors nonetheless. Most of us would probably feel a little sheepish if we were caught slurping a milkshake in our office; a Frappuccino, on the other hand, is a different story. The same goes for discussing breakfast with our kids—cereal is probably negotiable, cookies probably not.

This is why, when it comes to consumption, our category tags may be specious, illegitimate, even spurious at times, but it would be a mistake to consider them meaningless. On the contrary, they stain our consumption experiences in highly consequential ways.

The Sony AIBO launched in 1999, and as its engineers had anticipated, it had all of the flaws of a highly complex, state-of-the-art, early-generation device—it was prone to internal software crashes, it was unpredictably buggy, and it sometimes failed to respond to its owner's commands altogether. This, however, is where the category designation came into play. Because the AIBO was marketed as a PET, not a ROBOT, the behavior of its users took a rather unusual turn.

I wrote a case study on the AIBO in the early 2000s, and over the course of my research, spent a good deal of time observing owners interacting with their AIBOs. What was remarkable about these interactions was the current of affection running through them. Considering that these were folks who had just spent well over $2,000 for their devices, AIBO owners were an uncommonly forgiving lot. This was particularly evident when the AIBO failed to respond to an owner's commands; rather than get frustrated, the typical owner would simply chuckle at the AIBO's stubbornness, or make a doting comment about the creature's "individualistic personality." As one owner fondly remarked, "I never expected it to have such a mind of its own! It ignores me when I call, and can't even tell me from a ball."

Now let's think about this for a minute. As I said, these were folks who had just plopped down some serious money for a chance to own some seriously cutting-edge robotic technology. You would think that they would be relatively demanding in their performance expectations.

And yet it was almost as if the categorization of PET versus ROBOT had liberated them somehow, to behave in a manner different from that of early adopters of other expensive, high-end technologies. Sure, they understood that ROBOTS were supposed to obey their commands, to be functionally efficient, to be highly intelligent. But they also understood that PETS were of a separate ilk—they were disobedient and unpredictable, they were lovably goofy, they had minds of their own. And so from the moment they encountered the AIBO, they suppressed the impulse to make judgments according to the default category archetype (ROBOT) and instead allowed the alternative archetype (PET) to kick in.

───

The AIBO was what I refer to as a breakaway brand. Companies that introduce breakaway brands recognize that when it comes to consumption, our classifications tend to be both superficial and arbitrary. But they also recognize that these classifications mediate our consumption experiences in profound ways. And so they deliberately intervene in our process of classification, offering us an alternative category rubric to replace our default one. These are companies that say: *I know that you're inclined to think of this as a slice of* SWISS CHEESE, *but what if you were to think of it as a* FLYING CARPET *instead?*

To understand how pronounced the influence of

this recategorization can be, imagine if rather than developing the petlike AIBO, Sony had decided to develop a functional robotic butler with a humanlike form factor—a hulking, metallic, RoboCop-like android that looked something like this:

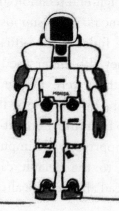

Now imagine that you were a technology critic for a major newspaper, assigned to write a review of this hulking android. You brought it home, gathered some friends around to help you test it out, and then commanded the ROBOT to walk across the room and turn the lights on and off. As your friends tittered in the background, you watched the ROBOT teeter a few steps, stop, whir . . . and then do nothing. What would you write in your review? My guess is that you'd probably skewer the product, maybe even chastise Sony for bringing such a flawed product to market.

By contrast, this is what the *New York Times* technology critic had to say about the petlike AIBO:

AIBO doesn't always respond to commands. . . . These displays of "attitude" are . . . scarcely distinguishable from "not working." [But later in article:] The AIBO is an impressive, entertaining and often joyous little beast.

Meanwhile, this is what the *Independent* in London had to say:

"Move back!" I commanded in a clear voice. To no avail. In the next hour I was to discover that this was a robot with a serious attitude problem. . . . [But later in article:] With batteries running low, I had to hand "Rolo" back to one of Sony's representatives. I must confess to a pang of regret. We were just beginning to build a bond.

Notice the tone of these reviewers. Both are acutely attentive to the device's flaws, but are also warmly approving of the creature's playful attributes. The new frame of reference—PET as opposed to ROBOT—has become an almost magical transformative device, transforming an instrumental product into a playful one, transforming a series of product flaws ("the voice recognition doesn't work, and the thing rarely obeys commands") into actual product benefits ("it's a pet with a mind of its own").

This, in a nutshell, is what breakaway brands are: They're transformative devices. By presenting us with an alternative frame of reference, they encourage us to let go of the consumption posture we're inclined to bring to a product and embrace entirely new terms of engagement instead.

———

In an earlier chapter, I made reference to the effort that companies like Kimberly-Clark (Huggies) and Procter & Gamble (Pampers) will routinely expend trying to manufacture the perfect diaper. What I didn't mention was that what's tough about competing in the diaper industry is that the customer life cycle is so short. Most parents like to transition their children out of diapers around the age of two, in part because there's a bit of a stigma associated with keeping them in diapers for much longer than that. Diaper manufacturers have historically found it near impossible to market diapers designed for older kids for precisely this reason—the resistance among parents (not to mention the kids themselves) to extending the diaper life cycle has been too strong.

This gave the folks at Kimberly-Clark an idea: Why not create a product for older kids that pulled up over the legs like ordinary underpants, rather than being fastened at the sides? The result was the creation of the "Pull-Up," a product that was expressly designed to distance itself from the DIAPER category by evoking the associations of the alternative category of BIG-KID UNDERPANTS. Needless to say, the breakaway was a success; almost overnight, Pull-Ups became the fastest-growing brand in the industry. Apparently, many of the same parents unwilling to keep their children in diapers beyond the age of two had no qualms about keeping them in Pull-Ups well beyond the age of four.

What's interesting about breakaway brands is that what they're doing is actually pretty quintessential: They are suggesting that we replace one mental archetype with another. They know that we're inclined to peg their product a particular way, but they also know how ersatz our consumption categories can be, and so they reinvent their product as a means of relocating it in a space far removed from our cognitive default. They present us with a ROBOT, recast as PET. They present us with a BABY DIAPER, reimagined as BIG-KID UNDERPANTS. They present us with exactly what we expect, redefined as something entirely different.

Of course, this requires no small degree of cooperation from us. In order for the breakaway to strike the proper chord, we have to "buy" into the recategorization. This is why a critical ingredient in all of this is transparency. Breakaway brands want permission to play with our heads. They know that we're going to know that the AIBO is a ROBOT; they know that we're going to know that the Pull-Up is a DIAPER. But they're counting on the likelihood that we're going to want to be complicit in the breakaway because we're ready to move away from our entrenched patterns of consumption. That we *want* to let go.

When HBO brands itself with the tagline "It's not TV," it's not only telling us that it knows we carry a set of (negative) expectations about the nature of television content, it's banking on the likelihood that we're ready to cast them aside. And so it is cuing us to expect something different to happen.

Perhaps a better way to think about these brands, then, is as representing a kind of invitation. These brands invite us to approach their products through the lens of alternative definition. They ask us to set aside our preconceptions about a particular product and experience it no longer encumbered by the weight of our prior expectations. And they do this not by trying to disguise that proverbial slice of Swiss cheese, but by directing our attention to how well it can float in the air.

———

One of the more popular works of fiction in recent years was Sara Gruen's *Water for Elephants,* a book notable for its visceral description of circus life. I've never actually been to a traditional Barnum & Bailey or Ringling Bros. circus, but while reading the book it struck me how well acquainted I was with the archetype anyway. The iconic elements of the CIRCUS—the clowns, the tentlike covering, the sequined animals, the ringmaster—have somehow become so ingrained in my brain that the book's setting seemed deeply familiar to me. I should add that the book only reinforced my inclination to stay away from circuses; I've always felt an aversion to them and the book did little to overcome this.

By contrast, a few years ago I took the kids to Cirque du Soleil for the first time and found the experience immensely satisfying. Much has been written about Cirque du Soleil, and I found all of it to be true: Cirque du Soleil carefully positions itself as being everything a CIRCUS is not. There are no animals, no ringmasters, and no peanut shell–laden floors; instead, the performance borrows heavily from the conventions of other entertainment categories—theater, dance, opera. It is a breakaway brand of the most deliberate type, and its earliest shows (one was called *Le Cirque Réinventé;* another was called *Nouvelle Expérience*) made this positioning as explicit as possible.

This begs the question, however: Why does Cirque du Soleil call itself a circus at all? Why not just bill itself as being an alternative form of theatrical gymnastics? The answer is that Cirque du Soleil, like many other breakaway brands, understands that there is a certain seditious advantage in being able to position itself as the player *in* the category willing to venture *out*-of-bounds.

About twenty years ago, the FOX network launched *The Simpsons,* a show that defiantly distanced itself from one category (CHILDREN'S CARTOONS) while associating itself with another (ADULT SITCOMS). But although the show was, in many ways, everything a traditional CHILDREN'S CARTOON was not—it was filled with caustic satire and irreverent cultural criticism—the fact that it was still a CARTOON was what gave *The Simpsons* its bite. The show benefited from being the player *in* the category willing to venture *out*-of-bounds.

Another example: In 1983, Nicolas Hayek decided to shake up the Swiss watch industry by introducing a watch that dramatically deviated from our mental archetype of the SWISS WATCH. Most of us think of Swiss watches as a form of high-end jewelry—meticulously crafted timepieces sold in the most expensive jewelry stores, made from the finest metals and jewels. Hayek's idea was to create a watch that leveraged an alternative category archetype—that of the EVERYDAY FASHION ACCESSORY.

The result was the Swatch, a breakaway brand that (to this day) remains the bestselling watch brand in history. The Swatch was a pioneer in so many respects. It was the first to splash flamboyant pop art designs on its watches; it was the first to enlist artists and architects in the design of its watches; it was the first to offer a product line consisting of collections that changed on a seasonal basis à la a trendy fashion brand; it was the first to retail its watches in mini-boutiques and freestanding stores. These marketing tactics were commonplace in the fashion industry, but unheard of in the watch industry at the time. And so Swatch was able to benefit from being the player *in* the category willing to play *out*-of-bounds.

In semantics, the word "differentiation" refers to a meaning shift that is attained by "adding concepts to original concepts." It is a fundamentally delicate process, because it requires holding on to enough of the original to allow for a meaningful comparison, and yet adding enough of the new to constitute a legitimate difference. In this regard, differentiation can be thought to operate along a continuum—it is possible to differentiate a little or differentiate a lot, depending on how much of a stretch you are willing to undertake.

A breakaway brand is one that makes the most of the stretch. It interprets the process of differentiation at the far end of the continuum, holding on to just enough of the old to avoid category defection altogether. It's the insurgent in the category, the boundary breaker. And so it gets to be and not to be, all at once.

———

In an earlier chapter, I introduced the concept of the category blur, and I made the argument that once a category becomes a blur to us, we'll start to adopt a consumption posture directed toward the category as a whole, as opposed to the individual brands within it. We no longer see the trees for the forest, so we'll cop a stance toward the forest instead. We'll write off BEER as being for football-loving meatheads, for example, or SWISS WATCHES as being stuffy and conservative, or DIAPERS as being for babies.

What breakaway brands do is deviate so exceedingly from our stereotypes that they cast doubt on the validity of these generalizations. They're like the cheerleader who gets us to take her seriously by getting rid of her makeup, donning glasses, and going to law school; they're the prominent anti-example that obliges us to reconsider the nature of our prejudices.

Put another way, stereotypes are misleading because they give us an average when what we really should be looking at is the variance. Breakaway brands force us to see the variance. And they do it by rotating their product so many degrees off center that we begin to see just how cockeyed our original preconceptions were anyway.

You could even say that breakaway brands *revel* in our stereotypes, since they make their living turning them upside down. We dream of someday owning a robot that will wait on us hand and foot, so what do these brands do? They give us a robot that *we* have to wait on hand and foot. We know that a watch is a product whose sole purpose is to tell time, so what do these brands do? They give us a watch that keeps time almost as an afterthought. We know that we're not supposed to pee in our pants, so what do these brands do? They give us some pants to pee in.

These brands are the antithesis of well-behaved, and their mutiny is directed squarely at the category assumptions we bring to the table. And sometimes the transgression is more than a touch provocative; it's a bit twisted as well.

What's tricky about categorization—even mindless categorization—is that it carries both the good and the bad of any mental heuristic. The reason we have a fundamental need to categorize is that categorization can be an enormously functional asset. (As Wallace Rickard put it in *The Onion,* "Stereotypes Are a Real Time-Saver.") If I know that Splenda is made from sugar so it tastes like sugar, this makes it easy for me to treat it like sugar. Sometimes I don't want to do much thinking beyond that.

And yet this is another reason why breakaway brands can be so effective: They don't try to fight our inclination to categorize; they understand that we need to know what something is in order to know how to respond to it. What they do, instead, is offer us an alternative category rubric that leads naturally to the emergence of an alternative behavioral script.

Consider, for example, what happened when Hayek introduced the Swatch. The firm did very little to formally educate us on what the new product was or how it should be consumed. And yet almost immediately, folks who became enamored with the brand began exhibiting consumption behaviors the likes of which the watch industry had never seen. Swatch lovers didn't just purchase a single Swatch; they purchased multiple Swatches to mix-and-match with their outfits, their moods, their tastes. They updated their Swatch collections as frequently as their wardrobes. Even those who had never shown any interest in the category before began buying Swatches by the handful.

The beauty of the breakaway, in other words, is that it leads to someplace familiar. We already know what FASHION ACCESSORIES are, so we already know what we're supposed to do with them. We've interacted with PETS a thousand times before, so we already know how we're supposed to relate to them. The simple act of reframing—from ROBOT to PET, or from SWISS WATCH to EVERYDAY FASHION ACCESSORY, or from DIAPER to UNDERPANTS—is all that is required to invoke the corresponding behavioral routine.

As a consequence, when we are confronted with a breakaway brand for the first time, we "get it." Immediately. Without prompting. Without reeducation. This is no minor accomplishment. At the business school at which I teach, one of the things we reinforce to our MBAs, year after year, is how difficult it is to change consumer behavior, particularly in mature categories in which consumption patterns and category stereotypes are deeply entrenched. But breakaway brands push us out of our rhythm of consumption, not by creating new rhythms, but by invoking rhythms that we wouldn't have thought to apply in that particular context.

In the 1970s and '80s, a breakaway brand by the name of Alessi began selling ordinary kitchen housewares recast as expensive sculptural pieces of art: Philippe Starck lemon squeezers, Michael Graves tea kettles. And people got it. Immediately. In the early 2000s, a breakaway brand by the name of Heelys began selling sneakers recast as roller skates. And people got it. Immediately. In the 1990s, Kellogg's Nutri-Grain began selling cereal reshaped in the form of a health bar. And people got it. Immediately.

Whether it involves getting people to eat breakfast bars in the middle of the afternoon, or getting people to coordinate their watches with their wardrobes, breakaway brands don't try to fight the flow; instead, they redirect us to a new flow, one that we're comfortable with already, so that we're able to slip into the swing without premeditation.

Along the way, these brands recast who *we* are as well. Think about it. Swatch recast an army of category pragmatists and reluctants into an army of brand zealots. Kimberly-Clark transformed a bunch of toddlers on the cusp of category defection into ongoing customers. Cirque du Soleil turned me, a category reluctant, into a brand enthusiast. All of these brands broke away, and as they did, they allowed us to break away, too.

—⁓—

When you take something that is familiar, whether it be a ROBOT or a SWISS WATCH or a SNEAKER, and you merge it with something that is equally familiar, whether it be a PET or a FASHION ACCESSORY or a ROLLER SKATE, it is possible to create something that feels new-fashioned in spite of itself. This is the moral of the mash-up: The mere act of symbiosis can create its own delicious edge.

In certain instances, this may be manifest in the form of an internal contradiction that somehow manages to forge a logic of its own. The first time I heard rap music with a retro riff, the music felt both vintage *and* fresh to me, and the contradiction felt right on. When I first tried my hand at blogging, I was struck by how inconsistent it felt to be creating a personal diary for public consumption; the inconsistency made sense to me anyway. I once purchased a Swatch so outlandish that I could scarcely discern the time; this was one of the reasons I liked it so much.

In other instances, it may be manifest in a contrast so disconcerting that it becomes a revelation unto itself. Let's face it, when a firm takes a DIAPER and conjoins it with UNDERPANTS, as parents we have little choice but to confront the artificiality of our consumption biases. The effect is the same as when we encounter a cheerleader with a Harvard law degree—the archetypal mismatch may rattle our brains a bit, but it can also create a bit of an epiphany.

This is another reason why I am drawn to break-away brands: They are a reminder of the extent to which the marriage of unlikely things—whether they be product categories, or musical genres, or personality characteristics for that matter—can cast new light on them, and cast new light on us as well.

———

One of the most well-known optical illusions of all time involves a sketch consisting of two images—a beautiful young lady and an elderly woman—embedded in one:

In an illusion such as this one, it is only possible to see one image at a time; to see the other requires a "perceptual shift," a deliberate and effortful refocusing. When I first encountered this sketch, I could only make out the young lady—try as I might, I couldn't locate the elderly one—until a friend of mine told me that the secret was to focus on the nose. I followed his instructions, and just like that, the picture transformed, and I could see the old woman.

I mention this because most of the products we consume on a daily basis are in fact polymorphous. They could *be* any number of things, and what we actually consider them to be is the result of a rather shallow set of historical conventions. Many sports drinks and many artificial fruit juices contain essentially the same primary raw ingredients, for example, and yet the former is considered a serious form of athletic replenishment, while the latter is considered a treacly children's indulgence. There are some energy bars that are no more nutritious or energy-producing than the average candy bar, and yet I don't know of many people who would consider munching on a Snickers bar in the middle of their workout. In each of these cases, the difference between what is being sold and what is being bought is interpretive.

Is the AIBO a ROBOT or a PET? Are Pull-Ups a kind of DIAPER or a kind of UNDERPANTS? Is Cirque du Soleil a CIRCUS or not? In each of these cases, the answer very much depends on whether you're focused on the nose.

If there is a lesson in this chapter, it is that in business, our category boundaries are neither immutable nor sacrosanct; they are flexible, changeable, pliant to the extreme. All it takes is a perceptual shift to enact a product redefinition. All it takes is a perceptual shift to transform the consumption posture of an army of consumers. Nicolas Hayek, the visionary behind the Swatch, was a student of the shift. So was Toshitada Doi, the engineer behind the AIBO, as well as Guy Laliberté, the street performer who founded Cirque du Soleil. All of these individuals were like the legendary filmmaker Akira Kurosawa, who used his masterpiece *Rashomon* to remind us that a story can have multiple facades, and that if we only turn the lens a little bit this way or a little bit that way, the plot is bound to reveal some unanticipated twists.

In the end, this is the signature of the breakaway brand—an utter disregard for traditional category definitions. These brands are in fact boundary defying, and by challenging our notions of what things *are,* they reveal how arbitrary our taxonomies are, too.

<center>~~~</center>

I have a colleague who likes to say that all business strategies are doomed to fail, eventually. The line always gets a laugh, and yet the point is a valid one: In business, it is unrealistic to expect any strategy to last forever. The best that a firm can hope for is a strategy that offers sustainable advantage over the long term—not over all of eternity, but over the long term.

What a breakaway positioning strategy offers is the opportunity to achieve a kind of differentiation that is sustainable over the long term. The Swatch is the best-selling brand in the history of its industry; it enjoyed the benefits of first-mover advantage for decades before competitors were able to chip away at its market share. Kimberly-Clark was able to dominate the Pull-Up segment for more than fifteen years after the product's introduction. *The Simpsons* is the longest-running sitcom of all time. As for Cirque du Soleil, it has no competitors; it remains sui generis.

In addition, these brands leave an indelible mark on their categories even after copycats emerge. In fact, this is what I tell my students: When you witness the birth of a breakaway brand, you are often witnessing the birth of an entirely new subcategory, one that is likely to alter the complexion of that industry well beyond the next business cycle. The Swatch gave birth to a new subcategory in the watch industry that today booms with fashion accessory brands ranging from Fossil to Coach. *The Simpsons* spawned a new television genre that eventually included *King of the Hill, Beavis and Butt-Head,* and *South Park.* Kimberly-Clark's Pull-Ups was responsible for the emergence of a new disposable training pants segment that today includes Procter & Gamble's Easy Ups. And so on.

This, then, is what I mean when I say that breakaway brands succeed in transforming their industries. They leave their imprint by expanding product definitions, by stretching category boundaries, and by forcing competitors to play catch-up for years to come.

Incidentally, a few years ago, I ventured back to Sony's laboratories. In the years since publishing my case study, I had been, on the one hand, saddened to learn that the AIBO experiment had been put on hold (a result of cost-cutting, apparently), but on the other hand heartened to hear that the engineers behind the AIBO initiative were still tinkering with the technology behind the scenes. The team had informed me that their latest robotic incarnation had a humanlike form, and so I was eager to see what they had come up with.

The prototype they showed me was called the QRIO, and what was most surprising about it was its Lilliputian scale—the pint-size robot was barely the height of a small toddler. Adorable to behold, it had obviously been embedded with some extraordinarily high-end parts:

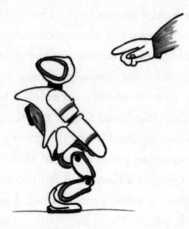

Nonetheless, the little tyke wasn't all that impressive from a performance perspective. It stumbled about a lot, occasionally knocking things over, and it definitely didn't do a very good job of "listening" to my commands. Still, I found myself strangely enamored with it—it was so cute and vulnerable in its appearance that I couldn't bring myself to blame it when it "misbehaved." I even caught myself smiling when it "ignored" me and wanting to "take care of it" when it fell. And that's when it occurred to me how effectively these engineers were, once again, pushing my psychological buttons.

hostility

one day in 1971, a young art director by the name of Harvey Gabor sat down to sketch out an idea for a new television advertisement. Gabor worked for McCann Erickson, Coca-Cola's advertising agency, and the spot he envisioned was both progressive and Panglossian: It depicted a throng of young people of various ethnicities, dressed in clothing representative of their nationalities, gathered on a grassy hillside on the outskirts of Rome, singing the words to Coke's latest theme song:

I'd like to teach the world to sing in perfect harmony;
I'd like to buy the world a Coke and keep it company.

The ad was released in the United States in the summer of 1971, and within months, Coca-Cola was receiving thousands of letters expressing enthusiasm for the spot, even as the song was climbing to the top of the American pop music charts. Over time, the "Hilltop" ad would earn its place among the most popular commercials in the annals of television.

The achievement was particularly impressive given the context: 1971 was a raw and discordant time in the nation's history. It was the year the *New York Times* would publish the Pentagon Papers, the year the newspapers were filled with stories of Nixon, Vietnam, the Black Panthers. And yet against this backdrop of social tumult and civic disaffection, Coca-Cola somehow managed to paint a tableau of unity and optimism. "Every age liked it," Gabor told a journalist a few years ago. "Grandmas sang it. People were singing it in the office. And kids liked it."

Of course, the advertisement doesn't look like much today—the lyrics seem hopelessly corny, the visuals stale and hackneyed—but that's only because the aesthetics of advertising have evolved over the years. The point is, what Coca-Cola was able to do four decades ago is what brands continue to aspire to do today: To wrap their brands in an uplifting message that somehow manages to draw us in.

When AT&T launches a campaign to remind us to "reach out and touch someone," or when Master-Card launches a campaign to underscore that the best things in life are "priceless," these firms are essentially breaking ground on the same emotional terrain that Coca-Cola so successfully built upon in the seventies. The creative execution may be more refined, but the branding logic remains as entrenched as ever: These brands want to throw their arms open to the world and make us feel good about each other, and feel good about their brands, too.

The idea is to melt our cynicism and seed a positive aura in its stead.

———

When I first began teaching marketing to MBAs about ten years ago, I took it as a personal challenge to inspire my students to think of marketing as the hospitality function within the firm. The analogy I drew was that of throwing a party: The marketer was the host—her job was to create the guest list, make sure people showed up, and then make sure they had a great time upon arrival.

If you'd have taken my class back then, you'd have learned that there were three spades to pulling this off effectively. The first was the product itself; it was up to the marketer to present the product in the most desirable light, to give people a reason to *want* to show up. The second was access; it was the marketer's role to distribute and price the product so that folks didn't feel like they had to stretch too hard to obtain it. The third was brand communications, the messages encompassing the brand. The Hilltop advertisement was a paragon because it so effectively hitched the Coca-Cola brand to an array of universal values: inclusivity, warmth, togetherness. This, too, was the responsibility of the marketer—to halo the brand in an irresistible vibe that beckoned people into the fold. In other words, it was the marketer's job to roll out the reception carpet and eliminate whatever barriers to consumption there might be, so that folks would rush to join the festivities.

The problem with this Happy Hostess conception of marketing was that, even as I was teaching it, I wasn't sure how I felt about it, myself. I never quite got the sense my students were buying it, either. Every year, I detected a palpable skepticism on their part, to the point where one semester I spontaneously decided to open the question up for discussion: So tell me, how well does this kind of marketing work on *you*?

Let me just say that the conversation that ensued was keenly revealing. For what became evident was that my students were one disillusioned bunch. And while this didn't really surprise me, what did take me off guard was the vitriol in their response. Their specific remarks ran the gamut. A number of students spoke about how companies were squandering their credibility by routinely portraying their products as being better than they actually were, by always "playing up the good while glossing over the bad." Others pointed to the inherent insincerity of advertising that so blatantly attempted to tug at our heartstrings—for no other reason than to sell credit cards, or long-distance phone service, or soda pop.

I've since had numerous variations of this conversation with my students throughout the years, and although the specific complaints may oscillate from one year to the next, the contours of the discussion seldom flux. If I may use my students as a measure, I'd have to conclude that this disillusionment does not bode well for the conventions of the craft. The Hilltop advertisement was representative of what my students sometimes refer to as "feel-good marketing," and today, some forty years later, it is not an overstatement to say that this kind of marketing blankets us. Our day-to-day existence is saturated with sunny marketing vignettes filled with airbrushed emotionality: Mothers blithely making peanut butter sandwiches for their golden toddlers. Hip-hopping teens merrily chowing down on fast food. Family members playfully teasing each other over their cell phone usage. And yet if you were to listen to my students, you'd get the unmistakable impression that this kind of marketing is only serving to feed our collective cynicism rather than provide refuge from it.

That said, a few years ago, as a joke for my class, I came up with an idea for a comic strip. The strip was called "The Hostile Marketer." The Hostile Marketer didn't give a damn if people bought his product or not. He was antagonistic, contentious, always itching for a fight. He was also a killjoy. If anyone dared complain, he'd kick 'em right out of his shop.

The gag was funny and the students loved it, but you know what they found to be the funniest part? In the strip, the Hostile Marketer was weirdly successful. Despite all of the reasons he gave to people to stay the hell away, they kept coming back for more.

———

This is a chapter about hostile brands. Hostile brands are brands that play hard to get. Instead of laying down the welcome mat, they lay down a gauntlet. It's almost as if the managers behind these brands took out a marketing textbook and added negatives to every sentence. In this regard, hostile brands don't market in the classical sense of the term; they *anti-market*.

Some hostile brands do this by being forthright about their product shortcomings; others do it by being evasive with their distribution; still others do it by disavowing feel-good promotions in favor of messages that are likely to repulse as much as they attract. No matter the stratagem, hostile brands erect barriers to consumption, barriers that could in many ways be considered tests of our affiliation. As a consequence, they create schisms among us, visible gaping schisms, in which brand consumption becomes an open expression of our fealty.

This is a strange mode of seduction, to say the least, and I should confess at the onset that this chapter will betray an ambivalence on my part. For you see, I'm still trying to figure these brands out. I owe a debt to my students here; over the years, they, more than anyone else, schooled me in the counter-psychology of feel-good branding and the counter-*counter*-psychology of hostile branding. And they did so in true dialectical fashion: For every Coca-Cola Hilltop story I would push on them, they would push back with a rebuttal; for every MasterCard Priceless campaign I would bring to bear, they would respond with a challenge. As a teacher, it's no small thing when you find your students taking issue with what you're attempting to teach them. When it happens, I've found it wise to pay close attention. And so after several years of treating marketing as the Happy Hostess of the firm, I now find myself making the argument that this kind of marketing is in danger of losing not only its potency but its plausibility as well.

What I learned from my students is that the brands they are most passionate about are the ones that don't suffer fools—the ones that aren't afraid to exact a significant cost from us, to turn hordes of us away. These brands don't compromise for anyone, nor do they bend over backward to make good with the masses. In an era in which we've been trained to believe that the customer is always right, this can play itself mighty arrogant, but what my students will tell you is that it can also play itself pretty cool.

So while I am still somewhat ambivalent about these brands, I no longer need convincing of how meaningful they can be, and how oddly refreshing, too. Truth be told, when I brought the Hostile Marketer gag into the classroom, it was a concession of sorts. Because what I was really telling my students is that I was starting to get it. I'm not quite sure I've nailed it yet, but I think hostile brands are onto something.

———

Okay. So let's begin this way.

Imagine that it is the year 2002, and you are an experienced brand manager tasked with the formidable challenge of launching a new automotive brand in the United States. To say that the launch is saddled with a few handicaps is putting it mildly. There is, first, the matter of brand awareness. Despite its relatively high-profile heritage in Europe, your brand is a virtual unknown on this side of the pond. Less than 2 percent awareness, according to your spreadsheets. There is, second, the matter of money. Your budget is a humbling $25 million, a trifling sum in an industry in which established brands will drop hundreds of millions of advertising dollars without blinking. There is, finally, the matter of the car itself. The biggest wart is its size: Once introduced, your car will be the smallest automobile in the U.S. market, a good two feet shorter in length than the typical compact car.

Meanwhile, Americans are in the midst of a love affair with big cars. You know this. Again, it is 2002. All around you, all you see is people buying full-size cars, gas-guzzlers, SUVs, crossovers, minivans. The diminutive size of your unfamiliar little matchbox is going to be a problem—there is little doubt about this. Even you have to admit that the pint-size runt looks miserable to cram into, its trunk too dinky for anything more than a six-pack or two. Your stomach churns with the possibility that people will write the car off, not even giving it a chance, merely because it *looks* too puny for practical purposes.

This strikes you as being patently unfair. It is your job to not let it happen. And so you debate your options.

The first would be to develop a campaign that does some myth busting, that counters the perception that the car is too small for comfort. Your research has shown that the car's surprisingly spacious interior always seems to impress first-time passengers, as does the amount of stuff that can be loaded into the trunk. This could work, you think to yourself—a campaign convincing Americans that the car in fact *feels* bigger than it appears. A second option might be to ignore the size issue altogether, to sweep it under the, er, pavement. The vehicle has a number of other delightful features—excellent handling, an affordable price. It is also a genuine exotic, boasting, in addition to its European breeding, a unique "bulldog" design.

You noodle both of these alternatives, but in the end, you find that neither of them does much for you. It's not that the ideas are bad, it's just that they bore you. You've been there, you've done that. And so you find yourself casting about for another approach.

———

In 2002, Americans were introduced to a new brand of automobile. The car was, of course, the MINI Cooper—a vehicle that entered our consciousness with one of the more impudent marketing campaigns in recent memory. Most striking was how the campaign dealt with the matter of size: it literally assaulted us with the car's miniature form factor, essentially making size the opening salvo in the brand's introduction to us.

I still remember the first billboard I ever saw for the MINI Cooper. I had heard some prelaunch buzz about the new brand, and while I had found the car appealing in a retro-modish kind of way, I had also figured the MINI to be an awfully tight squeeze. And so on that day back in 2002, as I was driving to work, the sight of that first billboard stopped me cold. It read simply:

XXL XL L M S MINI

The message was exceptionally combative. It was almost as if the brand were saying to me, "Worried this car is too small? Look here, it's even *smaller* than you think." I couldn't believe how in-your-face it was. Not long after, I came across another promotion in which the company had mounted a MINI on the top of a sport-utility vehicle, again as if to say, "Afraid this car is gonna feel dwarfed by SUVs on the road? Well, check *this* out."

As someone who spends her time studying marketing, I found the message remarkably rebellious. After all, marketers are trained to say good things about their products. What this means is that when market research reveals that consumers have reservations about some negative feature, marketers are trained to counter those concerns with reassurances. Or divert their attention away to other, more positive, features.

In this context, the MINI Cooper campaign seemed to shatter prevailing cautions. I'd wager that back in 2002 there were quite a number of borderline customers who, like me, found the car tempting but worried about its miniature proportions. Given this, what was radical about the campaign was that it not only failed to assuage our concerns, but it deposited them even farther down some continuum of tension.

This, to put it plainly, is what hostile brands do: They refuse to play the game of persuasion in its old-school form. They say the things that other brands won't say, the things that risk chasing us away. I suppose you could think of the approach as a kind of reverse psychology, but that doesn't quite capture it, either. When Tom Sawyer refused to let his friends paint his fence, he was attempting to depict the act of painting as more appealing than it actually was. That's not what's happening here. Hostile brands present us with their product, warts and all, and if we don't like it, *tough*.

And yet they do so in a manner that is somehow invigorating. As I drove to work that day it occurred to me how rare it was to see advertising so piercing in its candor. I later learned that MINI's introductory "Let's Motor" campaign contained other subtexts as well; the combined force of these unorthodox brand promotions amounted to a fantastically crisp renunciation of the big-car driving culture so pervasive at the time. This, too, is a hallmark of hostile brands: They tend to be refreshingly blunt, brazenly challenging us with the unflinching directness of their message.

The psychological impact of this can be bracing. When a marketer introduces us to a product that is easy for us to like, the introduction tends to slide off us as effortlessly as smooth against silk. But traction requires friction, so what hostile brands do is give us chafe. And they do it, not by downplaying the most contentious aspect of their product, but by enhancing it. They recognize that there is a certain kinetic vitality that can only emerge out of psychological discord, so hostile brands do what they can to sharpen the dissonance.

⁓⁓

One of the cases I like to use to make this point describes the market introduction of the energy drink Red Bull, a tale of entrepreneurial swagger if there ever was one. I'll often conduct a little taste test in the classroom when I teach the case, selecting as my subject someone who has never sampled Red Bull before. One year, the student actually spat the drink out; it tasted that awful.

What's intriguing about the story of Red Bull was that when Dietrich Mateschitz, the Austrian business maverick responsible for building the product into a global brand, was preparing to launch the concoction in Europe, he ordered a series of market tests to get a sense of how consumers would respond to the taste of the alien beverage. According to initial research results, "the thin colour of the new drink was totally unappetizing, the sticky mouth feel and the taste were deemed 'disgusting.'" The verdict from the research firm: "no other product has ever failed this convincingly." Mateschitz's response to the results? "Great!"

Along these same lines, there is a supermarket brand in the United Kingdom that goes by the name of Marmite. Marmite is a sticky brown food paste that is an "acquired" taste, so to speak. The tagline for the brand is "Love it or hate it," and recent television advertisements have included ones in which a blob of

Marmite terrorizes a British town, and a baby projectile-vomits on his mother after she eats Marmite while breast-feeding.

What you are seeing in both of these cases is a pugnacity beyond ordinary measure. Hostile brands tell us exactly what we're in for, and if we don't like it, they're the first to show us the door. This is why I'll often use the term "anti-marketing" to describe them: These are "take it or leave it" brands. They refuse to pander, they refuse to kowtow, they refuse to even consider the possibility of modifying the product to sand away the rough edges.

When Red Bull's popularity began burgeoning in nightclubs and bars, its drinkers started giving the beverage nicknames such as "liquid cocaine," "speed-in-a-can," and "liquid Viagra" to describe the energy-inducing nature of the concoction; they also started spreading rumors that the drink was made from bull testicles. This led some worried consumers to begin organizing a Red Bull boycott due to possible health concerns regarding its effects. But rather than try to stamp out the rumors or mollify consumer apprehensions, the firm stayed the course, never deviating from an underground marketing approach that relied heavily on unrestrained word of mouth to generate interest in the drink. The firm's attitude was: If Red Bull makes you nervous, then DON'T DRINK IT.

As I said, there are not many examples of firms so unbending in their approach. To be this inflexible requires a commitment to being *un*responsive to consumer concerns, to being *in*transigent to market feedback. And yet the payoff for this kind of inflexibility is a market positioning that is as unadulterated and as lopsided as can be. The payoff, in other words, is brand differentiation to the extreme.

To wit: If you Google the words "Birkenstocks" and "ugly," you will get thousands of hits, and if you listen to Margot Fraser, the woman responsible for bringing the brand to the United States, talk about the early days of the company, she will fondly recall how some retailers initially refused to stock the shoes because they were so hideous. But while the natural response for many companies in this circumstance might have been to consider remaking the shoe to be comfortable *and* attractive, Birkenstock never once entertained this idea, for it recognized that such a move would effectively emasculate the brand, rendering it as neutered as the countless other shoe brands out there offering footwear that doesn't stand for anything. Birkenstock stands for something. This is the prize for its recalcitrance. The shoe's ugliness is a statement, and it's a statement the brand wears with resolve.

—

An interesting thing happens when a brand confronts us in a manner so uncompromising.

Non-confrontational brands are easy to consume. They don't make demands on us, they don't make strong statements; consuming them thus becomes a way of folding ourselves into the crowd. No one is going to raise an eyebrow if we show up to work driving the same car that everyone else drives, wearing the same loafers everyone else is wearing. A good way to be invisible is to avoid making consumption decisions that stand out.

But when a brand draws a line in the sand—a line that we know not everyone is going to be willing to cross—it forces us to think twice about crossing it, too. The act of consumption becomes less trivial now; brand affiliation becomes more meaning laden. To wear Birkenstocks, or to drive a MINI, or to insist on drinking Red Bull becomes a bit more revealing than selecting the same old, same old. Hostile brands are statement brands, identity markers, and intuitively, we know it.

What's more, over time, a set of peripheral associations starts to accumulate around these brands, such that they become infused with a rich host of meanings. Today, brands like Birkenstock, MINI, and Red Bull are suggestive of entire social sects, whether they be granola-crunching bohemians, or iconoclastic small-car enthusiasts, or nightclubbing in-crowders. This is why consumption of these brands can be such a loaded affair: While conventional brands help us hide, hostile brands force us to show our colors.

These brands are not merely polarizing; they actively *summon* resistance. Which is to say that they cultivate friends—passionate, loyal friends—but they are equally energetic in cultivating enemies, enemies that they welcome into the open. When MINI runs an ad that says "The SUV backlash starts here," the effect is fractious, and no wonder: The brand is essentially telling us that it is hankering for a fight.

Marmite splits its website into two sections—one for those who love the product and one for those who hate it—and welcomes participation from both. There are folks who wear Birkenstocks and there are folks who make fun of the folks who wear Birkenstocks; the firm knows this and approves of it. In a recent interview in the *New York Times,* Birkenstocks' brand manager put it this way: "[T]he brand's strong point is its power to elicit both positive and negative reactions. That speaks to the larger cultural relevance of the brand. That's something I want to participate in. That's not something I'm trying to shake."

This is what hostile brands do: They flourish in the dramatic possibilities of polarization. They feed off the friction. And while it is true that luxury brands have done for this decades—creating social fissures along the prosaic dimension of wealth—hostile brands mark us according to a more variegated set of allegiances, allegiances that have nothing to do with anything as humdrum as our bank accounts. Hostile brands thrive in a more kaleidoscopic divide.

—

If you were to spend any significant time in Japan—a country with a gross national cool that, incidentally, far exceeds its economic clout—chances are that you would eventually get wind of a brand of casual streetwear called A Bathing Ape, or BAPE. Born in 1993 as a youth brand with themes derived from the original *Planet of the Apes* movies, the A Bathing Ape brand name is based on a Japanese phrase that means "to bathe in lukewarm water."

There are many ways to describe A Bathing Ape, but perhaps the best way is to be as indelicate as possible: A Bathing Ape is a pain-in-the-ass brand. It engages in a kind of anti-marketing that holds, at its center, the premise that nothing should be easy for customers, that convenience is for sissies.

I am not kidding here. Every product released by BAPE is a limited edition item, which means that if you see someone wearing an A Bathing Ape shirt that you like, it's probably already out of stock. BAPE stores are typically located in alleys that are intentionally difficult to find, and they often lack signage to indicate that you've found the place. Most BAPE outlets have a policy of only allowing customers to buy a single piece of any product, and it must be in that customer's precise size. Even BAPE's website is a lesson in unfriendliness: Visitors can't access the site unless they first download and run a standalone executable file. And yet, the brand's belligerence notwithstanding, there are few young adults in Japan who haven't heard about, or sought out, the brand. BAPE is the Hostile Marketer come to life in fugitive urban fashion.

Now, if you think about it, the psychology at work here is not all that mysterious. Scarcity stokes demand; we all know this. If you were to visit Sotheby's on any given day, you would find all kinds of folks paying exorbitant prices for things that are valuable for no other reason than they are one of a kind. Rarity creates specialness, perhaps even a little mystique, and in business, this is generally a good thing. It is not without hazard, however. Because there is a second thing that scarcity does. It makes ownership effortful. And when things are effortful, customers experience that effort as a giant headache.

One of the more memorable *Seinfeld* episodes from the sitcom's nine-year run was a show called "The Soup Nazi." In the episode, which was apparently based on the true account of a real-life soup proprietor in New York City, Jerry and the gang venture into a popular new soup stand on the other side of town. The place serves delicious soup, but there's a caveat: The owner (the Soup Nazi) is notorious for kicking people out of his shop if they don't abide by his exacting demands for lining up, ordering, and paying for their soup. Even the slightest deviation from his requirements results in the bellowed admonishment "No soup for you!" followed by banishment from the store.

To be a fan of a hostile brand—whether it be the Soup Nazi or A Bathing Ape—is to understand that you may be customer, but you will never be king. Instead, hostile brands present us with obstacles. The obstacle may be the size of a car, the uncomely look of a shoe, the inaccessibility of a store, regardless—to own a piece of the brand, we must be willing to incur the tax of ownership. We've got to put ourselves through the soup line. These are luxury brands of the non-monetary type, in which the equity of ownership becomes a function of the figurative price.

Earlier, I alluded to my ambivalence with respect to hostile brands. In some respects, these mixed feelings are to be expected. Hostile brands are intended to arouse dichotomous passions; they make their living in the love-hate collide.

I went shopping with my friend Laura a couple of weekends ago. Laura has three kids, two of them daughters between the ages of twelve and seventeen, and as I learned during our shopping expedition, both of her girls are enamored with the Hollister chain of clothing stores. If you're not familiar with the Hollister brand, you should talk to my friend Laura; she's got real issues with the place. As she observed to me that Saturday afternoon, "I don't think that store wants parents in there."

There is more premeditation to this than Laura realizes. Hollister does *not* want parents in there, which means that if you're anywhere over the age of twenty, the store is architected to alienate you. The place resembles a beach shack; the lighting is ridiculously dim, the music blaring, the walls covered with images of provocatively posed teens. But that's not all. The company also makes no secret of the fact that you shouldn't bother shopping there if you happen to be a teenager who doesn't fit the Hollister "profile." You see, Hollister, like its sister chain Abercrombie & Fitch, deliberately spurns kids who don't fit the company's definition of attractive, which is to say aren't skinny (specifically, that can't fit into sizes 0 to 9—based on a sizing chart that is deliberately sized smaller than standard). All the teens know this; if you're a middle schooler, you're either someone who can wear Hollister or someone who can't.

Now, the concept of a retail store that makes some children feel beautiful at the expense of making other children feel unattractive is disquieting, to say the least. For this and a number of other reasons that I won't go into, Hollister is a hostile brand that disturbs me to my core, as much as it does Laura. There are few things more disaffecting than coming face-to-face with the brand that stands for values that you distaste.

This, then, is the reason for my ambivalence about these brands: For every one I find myself enticed by, there is another that leaves me sore. Or to put it more directly, the trouble with hostile brands is that I don't get to pick which ones exist.

―――――

And yet here is another story, from the other side.

Not long ago, my younger son went through a stage where he started wearing all of his shirts inside-out. It was the oddest thing; this little first-grade munchkin who had never before shown any interest in clothing would wake up, pull a shirt out of his drawer, flip it inside-out, and then slip it on. When I asked him why he was doing it, he would just grin and tell me he felt like it. His brother would gently tease him at the break-fast table—*People are going to look at you funny. . . .* To which he would confidently reply, *I like it.*

When we are surrounded by conformity, by homo-geneity, we all look for ways to create a little chafe. To set ourselves apart, just a little bit. That's what I thought to myself as I watched my son going through this eccentric fashion phase of his. We live in a culture in which there really aren't a whole lot of ways for us to share our inner lives with one another, on the street and in the subway and at the store.

What hostile brands have in common with each other—regardless of the type—is that they are stridently, vehemently differentiated, for better or for worse. What this means is that they give *us* a chance to differentiate ourselves, for better or worse. They are like temporary tattoos, inking themselves onto our public identities, allowing us to reveal ourselves to each other, if only a little bit, as we pass each other in transit. And if they didn't exist, we'd probably *need* them to exist. We'd all look for ways to turn our own shirts inside-out.

But there is a cost to this. It is the cost of living in a society in which consensus is not mandatory: You have to be willing to rub up against people who like to construct their world in different ways from you. What this means is that there are going to be teens who wear Hollister, there are going to be teens who wear Birkenstocks; there are going to be people who drive MINIs, there are going to be people who drive Hummers; there are going to be folks who watch Oprah, there are going to be folks who listen to Howard Stern.

This is not necessarily a bad thing, however. When there is absolute agreement, there is not much for us to talk about. Hostile brands derive their energy from cultural altercation, and as a result they're capable of generating a kind of social discourse. The polemic may not always be a comfortable one, but I, for one, would rather inhabit a space in which the temperature occasionally runs hot and cold, as opposed to one in which everything has the same air-conditioned sheen.

In addition, hostile brands create divisions, but they create a magical kind of solidarity, too. I remember coming down to breakfast one morning wearing my own shirt inside-out. My little boy got such a splendid kick out of this; it was like we were part of our own little club that morning. When my best friend was living in Boston, she'd intrepidly wear her Yankees cap around Red Sox Nation, ignoring whatever jeers came her way. But if she just so happened to run into a fellow Yankees fan, it was as if she'd been reunited with a long-lost friend. Commonalities are always magnified when they emerge out of a context of feeling like you're in the minority; any world traveler will tell you this. In this vein, we take for granted how often hostile brands serve as a kind of social lubricant, mediating our loyalties in a manner that can be instantaneously unifying.

I am told that MINI owners will regularly share a nod of recognition when they encounter each other on the road. I've heard that there are nearly five hundred Facebook groups devoted to the defense of Marmite. There will always be mainstreams and there will always be minorstreams. Hostile brands correspond with the latter, splicing us culturally, but binding us together in subcultural ways. So although we may find our relationships toward these brands balancing on a deeply personal fulcrum—the hostile brands we love over here, the hostile brands we hate over there—it's not clear that we'd want it any other way.

There is one more story of hostility that I'd like to share with you, a story that brings our discussion of branding back to where we began. It is the story of Benetton, an Italian brand that sells colorful basics—sweaters, polos, denims. Think Gap with an Italian flavor. The story begins in the mid-eighties and early nineties, when Benetton embarked on a series of advertising experiments that quite literally took the marketing world by storm.

The first of these campaigns was launched in 1984; entitled "All the Colours in the World," it showed teens from different countries dressed in Benetton colors—not unlike the Coca-Cola Hilltop ad, really, just another feel-good campaign designed to make people feel good about wearing Benetton. Soon thereafter, however, the advertising took a heretical turn, becoming more reflective of what Luciano Benetton, the firm's founder, referred to as the company's "soul." Under the direction of the photographer Oliviero Toscani and tagged with the slogan "The United Colors of Benetton," the firm's print ads began featuring hard-hitting images uncoupled from anything the company was physically selling.

You may remember some of these advertising flights: A black man and a white man handcuffed together. An array of brightly colored condoms. A screaming newborn baby with umbilical cord still attached. This was followed by a progression of real-life photos torn from current events. A bombed-out car. A soldier holding a human bone. An AIDS patient on his deathbed. An empty electric chair in a U.S. prison. According to the company, all of the images were designed to reinforce the Benetton brand values: social awareness, moral outrage, political consciousness-raising.

Needless to say, the campaign ignited a furious debate. Critics like Bob Garfield, writing in *Advertising Age,* called the ads exploitative, a publicity gimmick, designed to "horrify the many in order to sell pricey T-shirts to the few." The nature of the criticism was telling—it wasn't that the campaign used images unmoored from Benetton's product line; firms engage in this kind of abstract branding all the time. It was that the themes the company chose to draw upon were so convulsive. They were divisive rather than inclusive. They were offensive rather than safe. They were jarring rather than of good cheer.

And yet this is precisely why, for me, Benetton is a noteworthy player in the chronicles of marketing: It was among the first global brands to turn the logic of traditional branding on its head. If you think about it, there are no rules that say the only emotions brands are allowed to evoke are facile emotions. There are no rules that say brands must remain detached from cultural agitation. There are no rules that say brands should not be permitted to claim a political valence. But as consumers, we've become so accustomed to having our brands delivered to us via a set of artificial images and saccharine messages that when we are confronted with one that doesn't hew to the mantra of unbounded positivity, we don't know quite what to do with it. The question is not whether the Benetton campaign was exploitative, it is whether it was any more exploitative than the countless other feel-good marketing campaigns we are confronted with on a daily basis.

Personally, I am still not sure how I feel about this campaign, but I do know that when I first encountered it many years ago, I knew immediately that I wanted one day to teach it. Because if nothing else, the campaign made me consider the Benetton brand in a new light. It also made me think, a little bit. It is rare that branding does either of those things for me, so on that count alone, it already had a lot of campaigns beat.

―⁓―

Branding has come a long way from a Coke and a smile. It used to be that the brands deserving of study were the brands that made us feel good, the ones that congenially welcomed us with open arms. Some of these were big, mass brands, while some of these were smaller and more targeted. But what they all had in common was that they embraced a kind of branding approach that the anthropologist Grant McCracken has so aptly coined minstrel marketing: the minstrel pursuit of the maximally agreeable.

Today, when I am confronted with this kind of branding, my reaction is not unlike that of my students. The display is too much and too little. In a marketing environment saturated with overblown promises and cloudless false reality, nothing dents.

Meanwhile, the brands I find myself paying increasing attention to are the ones that aren't afraid to evoke a more complex set of reactions. The brands that aren't afraid to put a stake in the ground and then force us to line up on either side of it. A student of mine once remarked that anti-marketing might just be the antidote for folks weary of being marketed to in the traditional way. I think that says it about right. We experience these brands with temperamental bipolarity, but that's only because we imbue them with such meaning. These brands create heat, dissonance, conversation. These brands *penetrate*.

difference

lately I have been thinking that there comes a point in
your life when you start to experience the full circle of
your upbringing. It is the point at which, when you look
into the eyes of an aging parent, you can literally feel the
relational pendulum changing direction, swinging back
at you with a force that you never quite expected. It is
the point at which it begins to dawn on you that being
the child of your forebears will never again mean receiving care, only giving it. My guess is I am not alone in
finding the passage painful to negotiate. To provide care
to a young one is easy; the rewards are in the here and
now and you get to taste them as you go. But to provide
care to an elder, you have to dig deep for the memories
to sustain you.

What makes it harder still is that the shifting momentum of responsibility can leave little time for
leisurely adaptation. You can't relax into your new
role, you are thrust into it, and the emotional physics
of the upheaval can do dysphoric things to your center.

That's why it is so stirring to come across offspring
who will, when the moment arrives, embrace the turn
with undiluted compassion. When I see this happen,

my admiration tends to flow in two directions: Toward the adult children, who have somehow found it within themselves to sketch the final arc of that circle with such grace and fluidity. But also toward those elderly parents, who have devoted a lifetime to providing the memories that have become, for their progeny, such precious sustenance.

———

Florie is a seventy-nine-year-old grandmother of four, an elegant matriarch with skin so pale and smooth it is close to translucent. I adore Florie; she is the kind of person who will touch your arm when she shares a funny story with you, or put her hand to your cheek when it is time to say good-bye. Not long ago, Florie's son and daughter made the decision to move her into a new apartment; you see, Florie had grown somewhat fragile over the last couple of years, and they wanted to move her to a place within shouting distance of their homes.

Florie was a little shaken by the thought of moving—she loved her old place and felt protected in it—and so in order to mitigate the trauma, her kids decided to make the transition as non-disruptive as possible. For them, this meant transporting her belongings in such a way that Florie's new home would be a near-perfect replica of the old. To tell you the truth, I thought they were a little crazy to attempt this degree of re-creation, but they were determined to do it, and after a frenzied week of measuring/moving/packing/unpacking, I'll be darned if they didn't pull it off.

The result was uncanny. When Florie entered her new place for the first time, all of her stuff was precisely where she "remembered" it. Her sofa here, her armchair there. Her photographs on the wall here, and here. Even her clothes were arrayed in the closet the way she had "left" them. Consequently, from the moment she walked through the door, Florie felt safe and secure. The familiarity was a sanctuary to her, bringing warmth and assurance to what she had feared would be unaccustomed environs.

When someone moves into a new home, it is customary to offer them a housewarming gift, something bright, something fresh, something to help bring the place to life. But as I watched Florie's children synchronize her move, I remember thinking that theirs was a gift that brought new meaning to the word "housewarming." Familiarity is the feeling a person gets when they experience sameness, and in this case, sameness is exactly what Florie needed. It took a deep empathy on her children's part to recognize this, and that's why their gesture was so befitting the circumstance.

The funny thing was, it also turned out to be a somewhat invisible gift, in the sense that Florie almost immediately forgot that she had been given it. Within hours, she was moving about her home so seamlessly that she at times seemed to have forgotten that she had moved at all. This is the flip side to familiarity: The comfort it provides derives from the absence of anything to stress about, which means that it is an overlooked comfort by definition. But Florie's children didn't mind; they hadn't done it for the notice. All that mattered to them was that their mother felt sheltered and intact. That she felt like she was home.

———

There is familiarity and there is change; there is similarity and there is difference. I've often thought that the sum of our existence could be expressed in this tidy way: As the old, spiced up with the occasional new; as the status quo, sprinkled with the intermittent variation. These two qualities seem to form the yin and yang of our experience. And although it is easy to regard the two as being opposites, they could also be thought of as complements, for their codependency seems manifest in just about everything that we do.

When we are overwhelmed by discontinuity, we hunger for stability, which means that something as basic as a photograph here, an armchair there, can provide ballast to an otherwise unsettled psyche. When I was preparing my children to start kindergarten, their teacher, Mrs. Selman, recommended that we send them to school on their first day with some kind of counterweight—a favorite stuffed animal, a blanket, a toy—that would help anchor them as they entered the scary world of chalkboards and desks and cafeterias. What Mrs. Selman understood was that when we are overwhelmed by change, a small token of familiarity can be comfort food for the soul.

On the other hand, when our lives are saturated with sameness, the overall effect can be desensitizing;

too much familiarity has an odd way of rendering things invisible. I have driven from my office to my house so many times that I can pull into my driveway with no recollection of the ride that got me there. I can walk through the front door of my home and the surroundings will barely register. Somehow, a lack of impression has turned into a lack of perception. This is the understated zen of familiarity: It doesn't so much provide pleasure as it removes provocation.

Ellen Langer is a psychologist who has spent much of her career studying a phenomenon that she calls mindlessness. Mindlessness refers to our tendency to perform on autopilot, without thinking, and it's typically the result of "over-learning"—of becoming so used to responding in a certain manner that we're not even aware that we're doing it anymore. When we act mindlessly, there is mental inertia even in the presence of physical motion. Langer probably wouldn't put it this way, but too much yin without enough yang can get a little mind-numbing.

What this means is that sameness is one of those qualities that is best meted out in proper dosages. I will sometimes play this game with my students where I'll ask them to ignore their assigned seating and sit in a different spot for the day, just to shake things up; it's my way of rearranging the furniture to make the room feel fresh again. Mrs. Selman has her own version of this: By the end of every school year, her kindergartners are so habituated to the daily routine that she'll take them on field trips, bring in classroom visitors, anything to counteract the doldrums.

When it comes to the unity of opposites, in other words, it's all about the balance. Similarity is stasis; difference is motion. And if the two happen to exist in dynamic equilibrium, everything is right in the world. We feel grounded, but we feel stimulated, too. We get our dosage of experientially bland carbohydrates, but not in quantities that would make us lethargic.

However, if too many days pass by without a trace of turbulence, that's when the listlessness starts to set in. We feel sluggish, we feel restless. And we find ourselves craving some strange fruit.

As it pertains to our world of consumption, I think it's probably pretty apparent by now that I believe that mindlessness has claimed the upper hand. Whether we are walking through the aisles of a store, or walking through the stores of a mall, we are surrounded by brands that fail to make much of an impression. And so, yes, we see that the sofa is there, the armchair over here, but with eyes glazed over.

And if I may go a step further, I would argue that this is always going to be true; that for the most part, we are always going to be surrounded by brands that fail to repercuss. Why? Because in business today, conformity is the prevailing standard. This is not because businesses are driven to correspond with each other; it is because they are driven to *compete*. And yet the effect is the same. Competition and conformity will always be fraternally linked, for the simple reason that a race can only be run if everyone is facing the same direction.

Meanwhile, the brands that manage to stand out from the blur—the brands that I have referred to as idea brands—will always constitute a minority set; the current of competitive conformity is too powerful for this to be otherwise. But because they represent the uncommon, the unusual, the anti-ordinary, we are disproportionately dependent on them to bring our consumption back into focus.

Idea brands don't try to compete. That is the key. They are more interested in separation than comparison. And so regardless of whether they engage us or enrage us, these are the brands that make us mindful again.

Moreover, they do so in different ways. Reverse brands do so by ignoring augmentation trends within the category. Breakaway brands do so by ignoring category boundaries, by challenging product definitions. Hostile brands do so by refusing to abide by the conventional axioms of customer attraction. Together, these brands provide demonstration that when we are overrun with sameness, there's nothing like a little difference to rekindle the senses.

That said, in the preceding chapters, I have presented you with a kind of typology consisting of three brand prototypes—reverse, breakaway, and hostile—and the problem with typologies is that they have a way of conveying rigidity, not to mention false authority. Neither has been my intent.

What I hope, instead, is that the prototypes I've presented will be helpful to you in the way that a newly buttressed vocabulary can be. We are now at the comfortable juncture where, if you were to engage me in a conversation about IKEA, I could open with the comment that it is a brand that seems to have executed reversal with just the right touch of hostility, and because you would know what I meant by this, we could dispense with the superficialities and plunge directly into a conversation about the brand in which both of us would no doubt learn something. This is not insignificant, I think. When language is properly loaded, it can go a long way in establishing the kind of common ground necessary for deep excavation.

This is why I'd prefer it if you were to think of my three prototypes as conceptual heuristics, as opposed to hard-and-fast specifications. Most brands, particularly the more compelling brands, tend to be Gordian by nature, which means that their complexions are always going to be more tangled than can be captured in a skeletal composition. This doesn't mean that we shouldn't try, however. And because we've established a shared vernacular now, it is my hope that this will only make any kind of deconstruction that much easier.

By way of illustration, consider the following brand: Apple. Throughout the years, it has consistently mixed-and-matched the various branding elements described in this book to forge an approach completely untethered by convention. It has been, for instance, a master of reversal, frequently withholding product features that can be found in other technology brands. To this day, a consumer purchasing a Mac must tolerate the absence of a two-button mouse; a consumer purchasing a MacBook Air must tolerate the absence of the standard array of ports; a consumer purchasing an iPhone must tolerate the absence of a removable battery. But Apple aficionados have always accepted these trade-offs, in part because the firm has supplemented these shortcomings with delightful benefits such as breathtaking product design and a gorgeous interface.

Apple has also been a master of the breakaway, repeatedly releasing products that transgress category boundaries. This was particularly evident a few years ago when it announced the impending release of the iPhone, its opening foray into the wireless phone market. If you recall, the pre-release frenzy had less to do with the fact that Apple was getting into the cell phone business and more to do with the anticipation that the product would straddle multiple categories and therefore redefine the smart phone space. Sure enough, the iPhone was a cell phone/iPod/browser hybrid that broke away from the genre.

Finally, the brand has been a master of hostility. Its attitude toward the market has always been that of *"You're either with us or against us,"* and the firm's long-running Mac vs. PC advertising campaign has given explicit voice to an adversarial debate that has raged among its followers and detractors for years. The brand has honed the art of alienation in other respects as well: It charges unfriendly prices. It is secretive. It is non-responsive. Its take-it-or-leave-it posture can pass as astonishing hauteur and it can come across as almost disdainful of its customers. But despite all of this—or perhaps because of it—the brand continues to captivate. In a commoditized category in which most consumers are pragmatists or opportunists, Apple positively shines, and it has hordes of devoted disciples to prove it.

What the Apple illustration suggests is the extent to which the concepts of reversal, breakaway, and hostility can be mutually reinforcing, and even synergistic at times. In addition, the brand's persistent magnetism is yet another reminder, against a sea of competitive homogeneity, of how utterly charismatic difference can be.

Not only is my typology far from definitive, it is far from complete. Difference can take on any number of forms, including those that bear little resemblance to my threefold scheme. I can't emphasize this enough: If you're trying to be different, confining yourself to a limited set of prototypes is probably going to be a little self-defeating.

To underscore this point, here are two examples that do not fall cleanly under the headings of reverse, breakaway, or hostile.

When most people think of Harley-Davidson, they think of a motorcycle brand with a down-and-dirty image, an image reinforced by movies such as *The Wild One* and *Easy Rider,* and historical associations with the Hells Angels motorcycle gang. Indeed, Harleys—or "hogs," as they are colloquially known—have a global reputation for being the vehicle of choice for rough-shod, hard-living outlaws.

But what most people don't know is that it wasn't long ago that the brand was in deep trouble. The threat had originated in the 1960s, when Honda had invaded the market with one of the most effective brand positioning campaigns of its era: "You meet the nicest people on a Honda." Brands like Yamaha, Suzuki, and Kawasaki had soon followed, and by the 1980s, it was obvious to most industry observers that Harley was being left in the dust.

This was a make-it-or-break-it era for Harley. Part of the problem was that the market had evolved and Harley hadn't kept up: Motorcycling had become a softer, less-threatening activity for mainstream riders, which meant that Harley's bulky twin-cylinder chopper, with its throaty growl and aggressive profile, was in danger of becoming a leaky and tarnished relic of the past. The company was close to demise, on the brink of bankruptcy, even as its Japanese competitors were coming on stronger than ever.

And yet in embarking on its turnaround strategy, Harley resisted conventional business reflex. Rather than succumb to market trends by modernizing the bike's design and softening the brand's image, Harley decided to cement itself even further at the other end of the spectrum by making a renewed commitment to the vehicle's classic 1940s and 1950s styling. It also decided to resuscitate its heritage as a nasty outlaw brand by launching the Harley Owners Group (H.O.G.), the formation of which allowed the firm to begin sponsoring rallies and cross-country rides—activities that were, in effect, opportunities for its customers to flaunt their Harley-branded gear as they roamed the country in entourages reminiscent of the dangerous and free-spirited motorcycle gangs of old.

What made the strategy particularly audacious was that Harley's own customer base had shifted in concert with market trends. The average age and income of the Harley rider had grown steadily over the years; the typical Harley rider was now an affluent forty- or fifty-something white-collar professional, "more likely to be practicing the law than running from it," as many company observers liked to quip. What this meant was that, on the face of it, Harley's renewed commitment to being the brand for the devil-may-care biker outlaw appeared to be completely at odds with the socioeconomic reality of its customer base. But Harley wasn't interested in reality; it was interested in reviving a fantasy, and this required constructing an elaborate mirage—complete with a ready-made H.O.G. club and a series of staged rallies—to give fresh incarnation to the dream.

When a company is caught ignoring the demographic trends within its industry, or worse, ignoring the changing profile of its own customer base, we're apt to label it as being "out of touch." Yet this is precisely what Harley did. In this regard, the sight and sound of a pack of Harley members roaring into town did more than simply refortify the brand's retro heritage; it created a weekend fantasy world so far removed from the actuality of its customers' everyday existence that socioeconomic truth was forced to give way to carefully cultivated mythology.

Today, if you own a Harley, regardless of how straitlaced a life you are leading, Harley will not only treat you as a true rider, it will give you every opportunity to play out the illusion. The result is a brand that is as close to a cultural phenomenon as you will find in business. With about a million members signed up to H.O.G.—by far the largest motorcycle-sponsored club in the world—and customers so loyal they will emblazon the logo on their own skin, Harley has taken the concept of aspirational biker glory to fantastical new heights.

Again, the Harley example doesn't fall easily under any of the three prototypes I've described in this book, but this is precisely what makes it so worthy of study: Harley figured out how to define difference idiosyncratically, in a way that made sense for itself.

———

Here is the second example:

Most brands in the beauty industry—an industry that includes soaps, facial cleansers, body lotions, hair-styling products, and so on—position themselves as selling the kind of aspirational beauty that we typically associate with gorgeous supermodels. They fill our heads with images of billboard glamour and runway radiance, and they imply that the attainment of this beauty standard can somehow be connected to the consumption of their products. The whole thing is nonsense, of course, but these brands are not unlike

Harley in this respect: They are interested in concoct-ing a fable, a fable designed to seduce, not convince. However, because they compete in an industry in which just about all the brands are doing essentially the same thing, none of them stands out.

This is what made Dove's most recent positioning campaign—The Campaign for Real Beauty—so ex-ceptional. Launched in 2004, the campaign set out to debunk the myth of unattainable supermodel beauty, and extol the aesthetic virtues of the ordinary woman instead. The mission was to bring the concept of beauty back down to earth, to make beauty accessible again. Note that this involved producing a set of adver-tisements that were completely prosaic in their ap-pearance: The ads featured everyday women—*real* women, not professional models—of all shapes and sizes dressed in plain white underwear. That's it. Just a bunch of normal-looking women hanging out in normal-looking underwear.

And yet you would've thought a bomb had been dropped on the industry; that's how radical the concept of normalcy was in this particular context. One indus-try observer, writing in *Brandchannel,* commented: "It may be more honest, but does its honesty leave enough women to dream?" Other criticisms carried a harsher tone, such as this one from *Slate:* "Talk about real beauty all you want—once you're the brand for fat girls, you're toast."

Dove's Real Beauty campaign contained other ele-ments as well. Perhaps the most prominent was a 112-second YouTube film entitled *Evolution,* in which time-lapse videography was used to reveal the false-ness behind the glamorous icons we see plastered in magazines and billboards. In the film, a rather ordinary-looking woman is seen being put through a painstaking process of cosmetic cover-up and photographic manipulation, all designed to make her look "runway beautiful." It's a biting exposé—the brushed-up face seen in the film's final shot bears almost no resemblance to the actual face of the woman who posed for the picture.

Both the ads and the film generated an immediate sensation. Soon after launch, *Evolution* became one of the most downloaded advertisements in the history of YouTube, and prominent personalities such as Katie Couric and Oprah devoted large segments of their shows to focusing on the issues generated by discussion of the campaign. Meanwhile, the women who flocked to Dove as a result of the campaign were among the most passionate the brand had seen in its fifty-year history; the discussion boards on the brand's website were filled with spontaneous fervor such as this:

> Around us, we see magazines and TV and movies telling us to be thin, to look like the women who are airbrushed beyond recognition. And yet, here we are, the real women of the world, and we feel bad about that! [My husband] loves me just the way I am . . . he tells me every day how sexy I am, and yet, I am unhappy when I look in the mirror. Perhaps it's time for all of us women to

look at ourselves the way our loved ones see us. I vow to do that, and I challenge all my women friends to do the same! We are women, we are strong, and we are loved!

What the Dove Real Beauty campaign revealed was how fatigued American women had become with brands that adhered to an unattainable aesthetic convention. Against this backdrop, Dove understood that in order to create something extraordinary, it needed to make its brand more ordinary. The result was a proud and glorious campaign in celebration of the mundane.

⁓

What I like about the examples of Dove and Harley is that they are two brands that created difference, but in diametrically different ways. Dove created difference by debunking fantasy; Harley created difference by nurturing it. And although neither fits neatly into my brand typology, that only underscores my point: Difference can't be concocted using preexisting parameters. What we consider to be different depends on what we consider to be the norm.

In fact, trying to define what is different is like trying to define what is opposite—the definition lacks content absent the context. This is why a framework—*any* framework—will never capture any more than a fragment of the potential difference out there.

This has several implications. First, it implies that the best way to locate difference is to simply look for it. Difference may be hard to pre-conceptualize, but it is not hard to identify. When something is inherently exceptional, it is going to stand out as a matter of course. To borrow from the words of the former Supreme Court Justice Potter Stewart (who happened to be speaking about obscenity, but you get the point), the property may defy neat description, but the subjective threshold couldn't be more elementary: You know it when you see it.

Second, it implies that there are countless ways to *be* different. As many ways to be different, if you think about it, as there are to be rebellious. Or to be creative, for that matter. No one has a lock on difference, any more than anyone has a lock on nonconformity.

Finally, it implies that although there are lots of ways to be different, not all of these ways are going to be created equal. In order for the difference to *make* a difference, not only must there be some kind of departure from the mean, but the departure has got to carry enough significance to be meaningful. It's got to reverberate, in other words. We've got to *dig* the difference, or at least some of us do. For difference to be charismatic, it's got to deviate *and* it's got to resonate.

━━━

When I was in high school, one of my teachers gave the entire class an assignment that we all had to complete in the same twenty-four-hour period. The assignment was to go for twenty-four hours trying to be nonconformist. According to my teacher, the purpose of the assignment was to give us a chance to reveal a more authentic version of ourselves to each other. The only ground rules were that we couldn't do anything that harmed or disrupted other people or violated school regulations in any way.

On the morning of the assignment, I decided to show my nonconformity by wearing a bizarre outfit to school, sort of a combination pajama/sweatshirt thing that made me look like I had just rolled out of bed. When I got to campus, I discovered that many of my classmates had gone the same route—they had used clothing to express their individuality; the hallways were filled with kids dressed in ridiculous getups. Others had done their hair up in extravagant styles, while still others had done outlandish things with their jewelry and makeup. A few had decided to engage in silly, attention-getting behaviors. I remember one group of girls holding hands and skipping through the hallways in between classes, laughing and singing like a group of preschoolers. I remember another girl, a gymnast, doing cartwheels in the lunchroom.

In retrospect, I guess you could say the exercise was pretty memorable. I mean, don't get me wrong, none of us *really* showed our true selves that day, or at least, I don't think any of us did. Looking back, I'm not even sure my teacher had expected us to; that's a lot to ask of a bunch of image-conscious adolescents. Most of us had simply gone through the motions, re-sorting to shenanigans that we knew would buy us a cheap laugh.

Still, there was one kid, a kid I'll call J, who almost singlehandedly made this a day I'll never forget. You couldn't imagine a more unlikely person to do this, by the way. J was a quiet kid, not particularly geeky but not particularly popular, either. Definitely not the kind of kid who ever called much attention to himself. Anyway, J showed up to school that morning dressed the way he always dressed, looking the way he always looked. But when he raised his hand during first period—I don't remember what class it was, maybe history or physics or something—he did an unexpected thing when the teacher called upon him to speak: He stood up to offer his reply.

That's right, he *stood up*. To offer his reply. And when he spoke, he did so softly, earnestly, respectfully. As if there was nothing more important, nothing more consequential, than this class, this answer. I remember exchanging a glance with the other kids in the classroom when it happened, a glance that said, *Is this guy serious?*

Next period, same thing. Whenever J was called upon, he would stand up to offer his reply. And each time he would speak, he would do so with utter sincerity. As if he really cared about the question, as if he really cared about putting some thought into his answer. And that's not all—he would address the teacher as Sir or Ma'am. He would address the rest of us as Mister This or Miss That. And at the end of each period, he'd walk up to the front of the room and shake the teacher's hand with a quiet thank you.

Now, the first time J did this, we couldn't help but titter, and honestly, can you blame us? The whole thing was so weird, we were all sort of expecting there to be a punch line. But as the day wore on, the tittering started to die down, because, I dunno, it began to dawn on us that there was something *awesome* about what J was doing. Something dignified, something mature, something maybe even a little bit brave. And he was so good at it, that was the other thing. He was so purposeful, so outrageously respectful in his demeanor. I can't speak for the rest of the class, but by the end of the day my friends and I had decided that the whole thing had been pretty righteous.

What I learned from this assignment was that there are two kinds of difference. There is a kind of difference that says nothing, and there is a kind of difference that speaks volumes. When I decided to show up to school that day wearing a quirky outfit, I knew that I wouldn't be the only one to do so, but I went with the easy gimmick because I couldn't be bothered to look for a more meaningful alternative. And so if I had to be honest about it, I guess I didn't really choose to be different at all, or if I did, I chose a kind of difference that ended up saying nothing. Not that I was alone in this respect; most of us chose to say nothing that day.

The exception to this was J. In that twenty-four-hour period, J totally reinvented himself; we all saw it. I'm not quite sure why he did it, maybe he really had something in him he wanted to say to us back then. Whatever the reason, J alone chose to speak volumes. And as a result, by the end of the day, my sense is that there wasn't a student among us who didn't hold him in elevated regard.

When it comes to grabbing our attention, there are always going to be folks who take the effortless and mindless approach. Who try to win our notice by being loud, or by being fatuous, or by wearing their floppy pajamas to school. But when this happens, it turns out that, if we are given enough time to think about it, this is what we do: We simply separate the folks who are saying nothing from the folks who are saying something, and the former we dismiss as not being that different at all. As for the latter, these are the ones for whom we reserve our full attention, the ones we hold in genuinely different regard.

The same could be said about brands, I think. There are always going to be brands that look for the easy gimmick or the attention-grabbing stunt. That try to court publicity by doing the equivalent of cartwheels in the lunchroom. But when this happens, it turns out that this is what we do: We simply dispose of the no-names here, and cache the remainders . . . the Doves, the Harleys, the Apples . . . safely over here. Because these brands deviate in ways that reverberate, in ways that *speak* to us, somehow.

―――

Florie's been in her new place for about a year now, and as you might expect, she's settled nicely into a routine. She wakes up, has breakfast, plays board games with her friends. Lunch, a bit of exercise, an afternoon activity, followed by dinner and then bed. She has become so embedded in her daily regimen, as a matter of fact, that her kids now find that they have to work a little to coax her out of her house. Monotony can be sapping in a different way than over-exertion, it seems. So her kids do what they can to mix things up. Her daughter takes her out to get her hair done. Her son picks her up for pancake breakfasts at his home.

Florie's late husband, Richie, used to joke that the secret to cheating old age was to stay a moving target. The older I get, the more I find myself agreeing with him. Stillness seems to have the effect of easing the senses, until it starts to dull them. So while most of us need our lives to be filled with a modicum of stability, we need there to be some motion, too, for no other reason than it's during these episodes of activity that we're able to feel our synapses firing again, sometimes even with the abandon of the children we used to be.

Florie's kids threw a party for family and friends recently, at a swanky restaurant in downtown Boston. Getting Florie ready for the party was a huge undertaking—it involved picking her up, helping her get dressed, chauffeuring her to the party, making sure she was comfortable throughout, and getting her safely back home.

After all that, I was the fortunate guest who got to sit next to her that evening and here is what I can report: Florie positively glowed that evening. She was radiant. Charming. As delightfully conversational as ever. And as we chatted and laughed and shared stories with each other late into the night, it occurred to me that with the passage of time and youth and vitality, Florie's personal point of equilibrium may have shifted further to the side of quiet, but this has only given such moments of punctuated stimulation more counterweight than ever.

I thought about Richie's words a lot that evening. Motion, change, difference . . . When all around us is a standstill, these are the things that breathe vigor into our lives.

part 3

the human
touch

(reflection)

marketing myopia,
revisited

the research behind this book started about four or five years ago with a simple meme about difference. We live in a cultural context in which we are surrounded by brands that generate nothing more than a bothersome background hum. Yet against this white noise there are a few brands that manage to produce meaningful percussions among us nonetheless, and I was eager to explore these brand acoustics in academic fashion. Now, bear in mind, one of the unstated laws of scholarship is that when you decide to devote a chunk of your life to studying something, you're supposed to have something definitive to say about the topic at the end, say, a new "paradigm" for thinking, or, at the very least, a set of hard-and-fast "takeaways" for business leaders and academics. Very early on, however, it became apparent that this wasn't going to happen with me.

Human behavior is complicated. I knew this going in, but what was humbling for me was the discovery that studying it doesn't make it any less so. To be an academic is to commit yourself to the search for fundamental truth, and yet what I learned over the course of my research was that when it comes to the study of human behavior, the truth can be an elusive thing. Yes, people are hungry for familiarity . . . no, wait a minute . . . sometimes they're starved for change. Yes, people are impatient for progress . . . no, wait a minute . . . sometimes they yearn for the past. Yes, people are desirous of more . . . no, wait a minute . . . what they actually want is less.

In fact, over the course of my research, I often found myself retrieving a chalky memory of an old cartoon short from many years ago. In it, a hapless bird hunter has gotten himself stuck in a boat with his nemesis, a crafty woodpecker. The woodpecker—obviously the smarter of the two—has cleverly decided to sink the boat (and thereby drown the hunter) by drilling a hole into it. As the boat starts to fill with water, the bumbling hunter frantically tries to plug the leak, but it's a hopeless cause because the minute he manages to plug the hole, the woodpecker jauntily drills another. After a while, the hunter gets so frustrated that he decides to stop and shoot the woodpecker. Not only does he miss, but his bullet—you guessed it—rips another hole in the boat.

I felt for that bird hunter. It seemed that whenever I was at the point where I was ready to declare that I had finally figured something out—that I had stumbled upon some unassailable insight into the hows and whys of consumer behavior—I was confronted with some fresh observation that sprang a leak in my not-so-watertight conclusion. As a consequence, the more involved I became in my research, the less definitive I found myself feeling, about everything.

And yet this is what kept me going.

When I was in graduate school, I had an adviser who was an absolute gem. Not because he was brilliant (which he definitely was, although to be honest with you, in the most marvelous academic circles even brilliance can be commonplace, so this definitely wasn't the primary source of his appeal). No, what made the guy such an intellectual diamond was that he had a way of looking at the world that was always off center, which meant that whenever he opened his mouth to speak, you never knew what was going to come out. Scholars are, by virtue of the necessities of the profession, cautious creatures, but this man was such an intellectual free spirit—so uninhibited with his ideas, so unrestrained in his thinking—that even when you found yourself disagreeing with him, even when you were convinced that he was actually quite wrong, this didn't stop you from listening very closely every time he spoke. He not only disrupted the way you thought about things, but he opened your mind to things you never would have thought about to begin with.

I remember once expressing my wonder at his lack of cerebral inhibition, his knack for unearthing strange and eccentric insights, and his response to me was illuminating. What he said was, *What liberates me, Youngme, is that I don't worry about being absolutely, 100 percent, right all the time. If my goal were to be unassailable, I'd have very little to offer the world. What I try to do instead is look*

*for the most interesting 2 percent I can find, and then provide
a perspective on it that people aren't going to get anywhere
else. The trick, Youngme, is to always gravitate toward the cool
stuff that no one else is paying attention to.*

Over the past four or five years, I have thought
about the words of my adviser many times. When it
comes to the study of human behavior, I have decided,
it's not that the truth is elusive, it's that it is liquid. It
comes at you from all sides, springing leaks at you
from every possible angle. What this means is that the
danger for the scholar is not in confusing what is true
with what is false, it's in allowing yourself to get se-
duced into thinking that it's possible to be definitive,
about anything. Because when it comes to human behavior, the truth is more expansive than that. When it
comes to human behavior, the truth is an ocean.

On the other hand, if all of us only dared to ever
speak or write or put forth the things we knew to be
unassailable, then we really wouldn't have much of interest to contribute at all. In the end, this is the lesson
that I took away from my adviser. When we are too
cautious about the things we are willing to offer, we
strip our discourse of any possibility of counter-
intuition, of discovery and of surprise.

This book is very much a working draft, which is
another way of saying that I have tried very hard to approach it with the same lack of self-consciousness that
I would feel if I were simply thinking out loud, on
paper. I think I've gotten some of it right, but I'm sure
I've gotten some of it wrong, too. It is a leaky, leaky
boat, this book of mine. Still, I have attempted to ad-

here to two deeply held convictions throughout. The first is the idea that there can be value in the skew. What I admired most about my adviser was that once he decided to focus in on something he always made sure to spin it around first so that he could speak to it off angle. I've tried to do this too, throughout the book; I've tried to come at things from a perspective that is, at the very least, several degrees removed from that to which you might be accustomed.

The second is the idea that there can be value in provocation, a kind of value that is distinct from the value delivered by a set of hard-and-fast business prescriptions. You will see this conviction, in particular, in the remaining few pages, where I offer a final set of thoughts about the challenge of differentiation in our culture today. To be clear, these are nothing like the kind of action-oriented business takeaways that you often find at the end of business publications. They are merely personal musings and random observations— my 2 percent, and a rather tentative 2 percent at that. But I offer them nonetheless, because I, like my mentor before me, am motivated by the notion that sometimes the best way to contribute to a conversation is to simply try to steer it to some of the cool stuff we may not be paying enough attention to.

———

In business, differentiation is everything; we all know this. In our business schools, we preach the importance of differentiation; in our executive suites, we build our strategies around the concepts of differentiation.

But we are forgetting what it means to be different. I use the first-person plural here, because I am as culpable as anyone. We all are, all of us who have anything to do with the way that business is practiced today, and that includes managers as well as academics. There is something wrong with the way we are thinking about differentiation. There *must* be. Because in spite of our verbal homage to the concept, we continue to produce brands that are notable, not for their difference, but for their sameness.

The disconnect is confounding, actually. I had a conversation with a friend this past week in which she mentioned, in passing, an incident that had recently occurred to her while she was staying at a Hyatt-like hotel. I couldn't help but interrupt. *Hyatt-like?* I asked her. *What do you mean, Hyatt-like? Was it actually a Hyatt hotel?*

Oh, I don't remember which hotel it was, exactly, she said and shrugged. *It was just one of those Hyatt-like hotels.*

I didn't bother pressing any further, because in fact I knew exactly what she was talking about. We all stay in Hyatt-like hotels, we all drive Honda-like cars, we all consume branded generics, all the time, you and I. And so it's easy for us, too, to slip into the slang of blurry sameness when we refer to these brands, in the same way that my friend did, during those moments when we find ourselves casually chatting it up with buddies or siblings or spouses.

And yet the instant we put our business hats back on, we are back to speaking the formal language of differentiation. As if we're not aware of any disconnect, as if we're not aware that there is a chasm between the way we talk about our brands and the way people experience them. It's no wonder that consumers think we don't get it. We tell them our brands are differentiated, when we both know that they are not. We are part of a continental drift, you and I. . . .

———

One of the reasons that this is happening, I believe, is that we have gotten stuck in a self-defeating cycle of competition. Or, to put it more forcefully, our competitive competence is killing us.

When I visit a company to interview its executives, the first thing that will often happen during my visit is that my host will present me with a pile of competitive analyses—competitive positioning maps, competitive benchmarking statistics, and so on—so that I can develop a better understanding of the firm's strategic thinking. The material is impressive, there is no denying this, but after years of watching managers put this data to use, I find myself left with the perverse impression that it is possible for us to know *too much* about our competitors.

Having a wealth of competitive information at our disposal is affecting us in at least two ways, in my observation. One, it is creating a kind of competitive myopia, whereby we are now spending a disproportionate amount of energy fixated on what our competitors are doing. Every last tactical detail, every last piece of competitive minutiae, none of it escapes our attention anymore. And so it is that we notice that Competitor A is offering a couple of new features in this market, or that Competitor B has raised its prices in that market. The commitment to competitive vigilance is well intentioned, but it can be distracting, too, in the same way that OCD can be distracting.

Our competitive myopia has spawned a second, related problem as well: It has created a dynamic in which our tendency to mirror (or better yet, to one-up) the movements of our competitors has started to become reflexive. I discussed this in an earlier chapter: Nothing generates conformity quite so organically as the existence of a comparative metric. When someone shows us a graph or a chart or a spreadsheet that displays the areas in which we are lagging our business rivals, it is almost impossible for us to resist the urge to play catch-up.

The result is a degree of competitive herding that can border on the nonsensical. Hotels allow guests to watch cable television for free, but retain the bizarrely archaic practice of charging a fee for local phone calls. The soap in the bathroom is there for the taking, but the soda in the minibar is not. I'm not saying that this should be any other way; I'm merely saying that it is odd that it is precisely *this* way, with so little competitive deviation, down to this level of granularity.

Thorstein Veblen was a turn-of-the-century economist whose legacy included the origination of the phrase "conspicuous consumption." In his most well-known book, *The Theory of the Leisure Class,* he contended that modern consumption was becoming an empty exercise in which all anyone ever cared about anymore was keeping up with the Joneses. Consumers were losing the point of it all, Veblen argued.

Recently, it occurred to me that if Veblen were alive today, he might identify a corollary phenomenon that could be referred to as conspicuous *competition*. When we spend too much time comparing our own brand performance to that of our competitors, it is easy to end up on a competitive treadmill. It is easy to wind up spending too much time keeping up with the Joneses. In the process, it is easy for us to begin losing the point of it all—which is to create deep and sustainable grooves of separation from each other.

Now, to be clear, I am not suggesting that we should be ignoring our competition. But I do believe that it is important for us to begin looking at ourselves the way that consumers do. When consumers look at the brands within a particular category, more often than not, all they see is a competitive blur.

The objective is not to blend into the blur; the objective is to stand out from it. This is what it means to be different.

——

What is intimidating about a commitment to differentiation is that it requires a commitment to innovation—not technological innovation of the sort that we can rely upon our engineers to produce, but conceptual innovation of the sort that we must take upon ourselves to birth.

And yet here again, we encounter a problem. It turns out that the kind of conceptual innovation that comes most naturally to us also happens to be the kind of conceptual innovation that comes most naturally to our competitors, which means that even in this domain, there is competitive herding. It's as if we have all adopted the same innovation framework, one that is overwhelmingly dominated by a reliance on what I have referred to as the concept of "augmentation." So when we want to steal a few customers from our adversaries, we'll bolster our value proposition through augmentation-by-addition. When we want to squeeze a few extra share points out of the market, we'll expand our product line through augmentation-by-multiplication. Never mind that this kind of innovation has become both predictable and easily imitated.

Meanwhile, we forget that innovation can operate in other ways as well, ways that can be far more effective in escaping the competitive herd. Innovation can operate, for instance, through a process of subtraction. We saw this in the cases of Google and IKEA and other reverse-positioned brands, brands that were able to take a category value proposition that was bloated in size and create difference by stripping away the superfluous. The counter-logic of living in an over-augmented society is that it is possible to generate value through the removal of benefits, as long as that removal is thoughtfully executed. This was the lesson of reverse brands.

Innovation can operate through a process of division, too. We saw this in the cases of MINI Cooper and Birkenstock and other hostile brands, brands that were able to mine the equity in our subcultural divides. We have a tendency to dismiss polarization as being a negative cultural force, but the truth of the matter is, an oversupply of consensus can be pretty hazardous, too, in a culturally neutering kind of way. This is why, when a brand makes it clear that it isn't afraid to take sides, we will often reward it with a concentrate of social currency. This was the lesson of hostile brands.

Innovation can even operate through a process of transformation. In mathematics, when you transform an equation, you alter its manifest form in such a way that the new equation remains equal to the old, except that it is now possible to solve it using an alternative approach. The transformation is superficial, but nonetheless essential to making the equation more tractable. Likewise, when a company transforms a ROBOT into a PET, or a pair of DIAPERS into a pair of UNDERPANTS, the effect is the same—the alteration of the manifest form doesn't invalidate the essence of the underlying product, it simply makes consumption of it more tractable. This was the lesson of breakaway brands.

In all of these cases, we saw that differentiation begins with nothing more than an idea that it is possible to do things in a fundamentally novel way. It begins with innovation. And innovation can operate in many, many ways.

—✺—

That said, in recent years, I have become increasingly convinced that great ideas, novel ideas, original ideas . . . are extremely fragile at birth. Why? Because in their infancy, these unfamiliar ideas are often indistinguishable from crazy, stupid ideas. This is why so many of them die a premature death.

Here is what I mean by this. Not long ago, I was scheduled to teach a session on customer loyalty programs—the sort of program that is common among airlines, hotels, and other service providers. Going into the classroom, I knew that these loyalty programs tend to engender a lot of resentment among consumers, so I assumed that the initial tone among my students would be sharply critical. And sure enough, once the discussion got going, it seemed that everyone had something negative to say about these loyalty programs, almost to a person.

However, after spending a few minutes dissecting all of the reasons behind their customer dissatisfaction, I asked them to put their complaints aside. It was time, I told my students, for a group brainstorm. The challenge was to come up with an idea for a customer loyalty program that had the potential to completely change consumer perceptions of what a loyalty program could be. A loyalty program that was delightful and gratifying. A loyalty program that was wow-inducing and buzzworthy. Complete the following sentence, I urged them: "Imagine a loyalty program that . . ."

It took a little coaxing, but before long, the ideas started to fly:

Imagine a loyalty program...

—that didn't keep score, that didn't keep track of "points,"
but that surprised customers with random acts of generosity...

—that, instead of handing out prizes to customers, gave customers
the ability to award prizes to employees who treated them well...

—in which customers could band together and accumulate points
together, in return for group-based rewards...

—that, instead of making it harder for the customer to quit our
service, made it easier for them to quit, without penalty...

—in which rewards were in the form of donations to the
customer's favorite charity.

And so on, and so on...

As you can see, the ideas were not only all over the
place but also somewhat hastily conceived. Which
means that, if we had wanted to, we could have devoted the rest of the session to ripping them apart,
listing all of the reasons why they were impractical, or
unfeasible, or operationally risky. And in fact, we initially started down this path. Whenever a particularly
unconventional idea went up on the blackboard,
someone would inevitably raise their hand to point out
all of the reasons why it wouldn't work.

But we very quickly imposed a rule. And the rule
was, for the remainder of the exercise, the only permissible comments would be positive comments,
comments that built on the suggestions posted on the
blackboard. And wouldn't you know it, the energy
level in the classroom started to pick up, almost

immediately. The students started championing their favorite ideas. They began brainstorming marketing campaigns. They began thinking up possible solutions to the implementation challenges. They began seeing the potential in proposals that they had originally been inclined to laugh at.

As I told my students that day, a curious thing happens when you decide to eliminate skepticism as an option, even if only for a few minutes: You give improbabilities an opportunity to transform into possibilities. You give unconventional ideas a chance to bloom a little bit. My students saw this for themselves: By the end of the session, their enthusiasm for some of their own ideas was palpable, their excitement contagious.

And while the objective of the exercise was not to communicate that firms should spend all of their time chasing harebrained ideas, the exercise did manage to illustrate a point about the fragility of unpolished ideas. Great ideas, novel ideas, original ideas . . . are tenuous at birth. And the reason for this is that, early on, they are often indistinguishable from crazy, impractical ideas. This is why, as I said to my students at the end of class that day, if we want innovation to happen, we need to suspend our disbelief enough to let it happen.

Not indefinitely, of course. There comes a time when we need to allow the practical side of our brain to have its say. But strange and unusual ideas need a cocoon, at least in the earliest stages of their infancy, if they are to have a fighting chance of survival. If twenty years ago, you would've presented me with an idea for a furniture store that asked people to construct their furniture themselves, I most likely would've laughed and likened the idea to a restaurant that asked diners to cook their own meals. When we observe a brand like IKEA or A Bathing Ape or Dove or Harley in full glory, we need to remind ourselves that what we are seeing is an idea come to life, an idea that probably looked pretty dubious at its inception. If we want to build organizations in which innovation happens, we need to create environments in which we are comfortable suspending our disbelief enough to let it happen. Or, as I told my students, we need to give our most unconventional ideas a chance to breathe a little bit, before subjecting them to the scrutiny of the naysaying sides of our brains.

———

If there is one thing that most of the idea brands described in this book have in common, it is that their differentiation strategies were not driven by formal market research. This is telling, I think. In business, we have somehow acquiesced to the notion that to invest in lots of formal market research is to be customer focused, whereas to neglect to invest in formal market research is to be irresponsibly inattentive to the voice of the customer. And yet it is difficult to imagine the kind of formal market research that would have predicted that people would fall in love with an energy drink that not only tasted terrible but was rumored to be made from bull testicles. Or the kind of formal market research that would have predicted that people would fall in love with a search engine that had not only zero brand recognition but far fewer features than its powerhouse competitors.

We allow this kind of formal market research to seduce us nevertheless. Consequently, we are more committed than ever to gathering it, using surveys or focus groups or customer interviews. We are more committed than ever to aggregating it, in the form of PowerPoint presentations and executive summaries. We are more committed than ever to drawing conclusions from it, conclusions that typically lead to some kind of renovation of our existing value proposition. And yet, as I noted in an earlier chapter, renovation is not the same thing as innovation, and there are times when I wonder whether we wouldn't be better off putting our marketing machinery aside for a few minutes, just to see what we're capable of coming up with without it.

I know that I am not the first to point this out, but here is the problem with formal market research. Consumers will always be able to tell us how much better they'd like our products to be. But we cannot expect them to be able to tell us how different those products could be. And more important, we cannot expect them to be able to tell us how it might be possible for us to surprise them.

What this means is that if we want to move beyond the incremental kinds of augmentations that dominate our product marketing activity, we need to look beyond the granular pieces of data that our market research infrastructure is likely to generate. Those pieces may be rigorously objective, but they are guaranteed to be woefully incomplete. They will only give us half the story. To get the other half, we need to take responsibility for the hard work of imagination ourselves.

One of the bestselling books of 2003 was Michael Lewis's *Moneyball,* which made the charged case that the right way to think about baseball was through the lens of extreme empiricism. The book was a slap in the face to baseball purists, because the implication was that the collective wisdom of a whole crew of baseball traditionalists—coaches, scouts, general managers, and so on—couldn't hold a candle to a statistician with a laptop.

In the polemic that followed the book's publication, what became clear was that there are two ways of capturing reality—by the things that are measurable, and by the things that are not—and because the two don't overlap very much, it is easy for proponents of either to diminish the significance of the other.

And yet this is precisely why it can be such a fascinating experience to sit down and watch a really important baseball game—say, the seventh game of the World Series—with a hard-core baseball fan. The hard-core baseball fan is a walking repository of a vast amount of statistical data. She can tick off batting percentages, on-base percentages, runs batted in, and walk-to-strikeout ratios. She can tell you whether a pitch was an outside cut fastball or an inside curve, and what the odds are that this hitter will be able to get on base against that pitcher, in this given situation.

At the same time, the insight that the hard-core baseball fan can bring to a game can go far beyond that which can be expressed in purely statistical terms. When it comes to a big game like the seventh game of the World Series, the hard-core fan understands the journey that each team has traveled to arrive at this place, at this time. She knows the personalities of each and every player, and is aware of the individual obstacles each has had to overcome to be in this coveted position. For the hard-core fan, the drama is not just in what is happening in the moment, it is in the collision of the present against all that has taken place in the past. Statistics count for something, certainly, but so do a lot of other things. Like context. Chemistry. Momentum. History. The beauty of the game. Which means that for the hard-core fan, to reduce the game to that which can be measured is to lose a lot.

I realize that I risk repeating myself here, but I draw this analogy as a way of illustrating the observational myopia that an over-reliance on empirics can create. As businesspeople, we can't afford to disregard the data that market research presents us with; we need to gather it, sift through it, and try to make sense of it as best we can. However, once we have done so, we can't assume that our work is done.

Much better that we approach our craft in the same way that a baseball purist approaches the game. Wherein we respect that statistics matter, but we also respect the fact that to reduce the game to numbers alone is to divest it of its soul.

If we only pay attention to things that we can measure, we will only pay attention to the things that are easily measurable. And in the process, we will miss a lot.

—*m*—

Idea brands are not perfect brands. Far from it. They are polarizing brands. They are lopsided brands. They are brands that are devoted to the skew. But because they do such an exquisite job of capturing our contradictions, they end up teaching us lessons about the inadequacies of our reductionist tools, lessons that they play back to us in fabulous style.

Harley is the motorcycle brand for the well-to-do, white-collar "biker outlaw." Dove is the beauty brand for the woman who is tired of trying to be beautiful. Apple is the user-friendly brand that carries itself with breathtaking arrogance. All of these brands lack internal consistency, and yet it is precisely this characteristic that gives them such resonance. They defy reductionist logic in the same way that *we* defy reductionist logic, in the same way that our own internal lives are marked by multiple and contradictory truths that transverse and bisect, that clash and combine, that create asymmetries and crosscurrents extending in every which direction.

Indeed, if there is a thread that runs throughout this book, it is that the consistencies of consumption, of behavior, of culture, are collapsing all around us. A brand can be hostile and magnetic at the same time. A person can be satisfied and restless at the same time. A relationship can be frustrating and fulfilling, can be symbiotic and liberating, at the same time. Of course, we already know this. We *live* this. I love my husband all the while he makes me crazy.

This, in fact, is what makes us so remarkable, you and me. We don't need internal consistency in order to cohere. We understand that our truths are too many and our lives are too short to subject to a set of neat and orderly constraints.

Well, idea brands seem to understand this, too. They may not make much sense on paper, but they make perfect sense to us. These brands bask in our discontinuities and celebrate our complications. They present us with irrational delights and counter-logical propositions. And in the process, they set a new standard of consumer insight, of customer focus, and of human understanding.

sign-off

i wanted to write this book because I believe that there are pieces of our business core that are simply broken. There are assumptions embedded in our competitive practices simply crying out for reimagination.

To be a business professional in this day and age is to be awash in things to *do*. There are product lines to manage and distribution systems to be tamed; there are pricing algorithms to refine and merchandising metrics to be met. The world moves fast and so we run *hard,* scrambling to stay on top of the machinery that makes it all hum. And yet as I've described in the previous pages, in all too many cases, the end result of all of this sound and fury is nothing more than a herdlike incrementalism, a kind of incrementalism that seldom manages to achieve distinction, of any sort.

I wanted to write this book because I believe we can do better than this. Not by doing *more,* but by being more thoughtful about what it is that we do. I try to remind my class of this at every turn. Differentiation is not a tactic. It's not a flashy advertising campaign; it's not a sparkling new feature set. It's not a laminated frequent buyer card or a money-back guarantee. Differentiation is a way of *thinking*. It's a mindset. It's a commitment. A commitment to engage with people—not in a manner to which they are merely unaccustomed, but in a manner that they will value, respect, and yes, perhaps even celebrate.

I remember reading once that the late comedian George Carlin used to hate it whenever anyone labeled him a cynic; whenever anyone did, he would correct them by referring to himself as a "disappointed idealist." The distinction was important to him, and I get it. To be an idealist is to hold tight to the belief that regardless of how jaded an environment has become, there is still a place and maybe even a reward for someone who chooses to play to a different standard. When it comes to business, this is how I would characterize my own thinking. The only reason that words like "marketing" and "branding" and "selling" have any significance at all in our lives is that, for better or worse, we live in a culture in which consumption itself has significance. Idea brands resound with meaning, and in the end, this is why they matter. They play to a different standard, and when they do, we *respond*.

I wanted to write this book because I believe that there will always be a muddied herd in business—in every category, in every industry, an indistinguishable cluster of brands moving in lockstep with one another—but at the same time I believe there will always be exceptions, too. The writer-physician Atul Gawande has written about the phenomenon of "positive deviants" in the medical profession, that small set of players who are mired in the same environmental conditions as everyone else but stubbornly refuse to allow themselves to be constrained by conventional wisdoms, and as a consequence are able to identify fresh and often counter-traditional ways to address seemingly intractable problems. In business, I believe that there will always be positive deviants, brands that are exceptional, not because they are able to run harder or faster than the rest, but because at some fundamental level they have made a commitment to not taking the status quo for granted.

Along these lines, one of the final assignments I will sometimes give my students near the end of the term is one in which I ask them to try to envision the idea brands of tomorrow. *What will these brands look like?* I ask them. *What are the characteristics that these brands will share?*

As you might imagine, the papers I get back are wonderful, not just in their thoughtfulness but in their flights of fancy as well. Some of them are filled with highly inventive visions of how consumption trends will evolve over the next twenty years, while others brim with more tightly constructed prognostications that pertain to specific product categories, such as fashion or hotels or carbonated soda. I typically bring excerpts of their papers into the classroom so that we can talk about them together, and at the end of this discussion, there is usually a moment at which the students begin to direct the question back to me. *What do you think the idea brands of tomorrow are going to look like? What characteristics do you think these brands will share?*

Like them, I cannot pretend to have a crystal ball.

Nonetheless, like them, I find it indeed fun to specu-late. And so here is what I tell them.

———

The first characteristic that I think these brands will share is that *they will offer something that is hard to come by.* Historically, the best way for a business to provide value has always been to offer something that is hard to come by. Scarcity always whets demand.

The question is, in an age in which consumers can choose among a proliferation of products and services that exceeds anything they could ever want or need, what is there *left* that is scarce?

Think about this for a minute. What has become scarce for you?

Personally speaking, I know that whenever I find myself soaked in an abundance of something—of *any-thing,* really—the overkill stokes a deep hunger for relief. What this means is that when I am surrounded by clamor and excitement and activity and commo-tion, what becomes scarce for me is . . . quiet. When I am besieged with choices and salespeople and offers of instant gratification, what becomes scarce for me is . . . a little time to think it over. Pragmatism awak-ens my appetite for fantasy; an overload of fantasy stirs a craving for the facts.

There is an opportunity here, there is an opportu-nity always, for brands to create value by offering a break from that which is profuse. This is what I tell my students. Hostile brands, reverse brands, the Harleys and the Doves . . . what all of these brands have in common is that they are mindful of what we have in abundance, and then they tender us something that is scarce. Remember: Restraint can be the new desire. A whisper can be the new shout. If there is one thing I feel pretty sure about, it is that there will always be a place for brands offering something that is hard to come by.

———

The second characteristic that I think these brands will share is that *they will reflect a commitment to a big idea.* Which is to say that they won't just be different in a little way, they will be different in a big way.

It is hard to believe that it has been more than twenty-five years since Ted Levitt introduced us to the concept of "the marketing imagination." Regrettably, a phrase that used to capture so lyrically the heart and soul of business has today taken on ironic undertones. We are now living in an era in which it is possible for an individual to experience an entire career in business without being asked to come up with a single Big Idea—that is, without ever being asked to exercise that imagination, not even *once,* over the span of a multi-year career. Whenever I teach in one of the executive education programs we offer at our school, the first time I use words like "imagination" or "creativity" in the classroom, I have to fight the urge to feel sheepish about it; this is the extent to which modern business has become detached from the good old-fashioned notion of idea generation.

On the other hand, here is why children are such

creative geniuses: Because they aren't as old as we are, which means that they aren't as experienced and they aren't as rational, either. And this liberates them, to approach the world without prejudice. And so they will look at a Tupperware bowl and they will see a miniature boat; they will be handed a silver spoon and their first thought is to dig with it. To be occasionally inspired is one thing; to be chronically inspired is another. Children are chronically inspired, for the simple reason that they aren't bound by well-worn mental heuristics, they aren't encumbered by habit or convention or the arbitrary rules of propriety. They are mischievous and subversive; they heed their inventive impulses, even as we have been trained to suppress ours.

Difference is deviance. Difference is permutation. Difference is a commitment to the unprecedented, which is another way of saying it is a commitment to letting go. If I had to make a prediction, I would say that the idea brands of tomorrow will be the ones that embrace this, even as they take that sharp left down that unpaved road.

―――

The third characteristic that I think these brands will share is that *they will be intensely human*. Which is to say that they will have been conceived by individuals who are acutely sensitive to the complexities of the human spirit.

This, in particular, is where I believe that we marketers must play a leading role. To be a marketer is to be the human touch within the firm. As marketers, it is our job to render our organizations human. What this means is that we need to be engaged with consumers—with *real* people—at a level at which the rest of the firm is not capable. If our organizations are fixated on engineering, we need to be focused on nuance. If our organizations are obsessed with the hard, we need to advocate for the soft. John Naisbitt once noted that intuition becomes increasingly valuable in the new information society precisely because there is so much data. As marketers, this is our responsibility: to make sure that our organizations capture, respect, and celebrate the full spectrum of the human experience, with all of its context and imagination.

Of course, in order to do this, we need to be *in* the world. There is oxygen all around us, and we need to be breathing it. From the clubs to the streets to the kitchens to the schools, from New York to Tokyo . . . we need to be breathing it.

But if we do so, and we do so deeply and thoughtfully, this will be our reward: We will discover that there is something to be learned from conspicuous consumption, just as there is something to be learned from closet consumption, and from non-consumption, and from hyper-consumption, too. We will discover that consumption can be satisfying, but it can also be grudging. Consumption can be careless. It can be political. It can be shameful. It can be competitive. It can be a badge. It can be many, many things. But it is always, always illuminating.

Differentiation is not a tactic. It is a way of thinking. It is a mindset, a mindset that comes from listening and observing and absorbing and respecting. Most of all, it is a commitment. A commitment to engage with people in a manner that reveals to them that, yes, we *get* it.

More to come, no doubt.

addendum

(NOTES AND OTHER MISCELLANY ON SOME OF
THE BRANDS MENTIONED IN THIS BOOK)

Whenever I give talks or lectures on my research, I am often asked to provide additional information on the brands I happen to mention in passing. For those of you interested in learning more about the ones mentioned in this book, I've provided some additional tidbits below. I've written detailed case studies on some of these businesses; in these instances, references to the full case studies are also included below.

VOSS / FIJI Water (pages 64–65)

The bottled water industry is a fascinating one to follow; I've always believed that there are few circumstances that make the businessperson's job more difficult than having to compete against an alternative that is not only free but ubiquitous (in this case, tap water). For evidence of this, one only has to look at how the music recording industry has struggled against the post-Napster epidemic of online music sharing.

To get a sense of how crazy the bottled water market has become, consider that in the 1980s, bottled water was still a relatively niche category in the United States, dominated by just two brands: Perrier and Evian. Today, there are close to a thousand (that's right, a thousand) brands competing in the $11 billion U.S. bottled water market. The proliferation in this category has been relentless: You can now purchase fla-vored water (lemon, lime, etc.); enhanced water containing functional ingredients such as calcium, fluorides, or vitamins; and exotic varieties containing ingredients such as oxygen. There are brands of water targeted toward pets; there are brands that claim a social purpose. And there are brands fea-turing new forms of packaging—lunch box–compatible sizes for kids, sports caps for athletes.

FIJI is one of the more recent stars among the "premium" waters. Positioned as an exotic artesian water from the "far away" edge of a rain forest on the Fiji Islands, it took FIJI just five years to grow into the second-largest imported water brand in the United States (topped only by Evian).

VOSS, by contrast, considers itself an "ultra-premium" brand. It was founded by Ole Christian Sandberg, a shrewd young Norwegian entrepreneur who was convinced that it was possible to sell bottled water as a luxury product in the United States. The story of the development of this brand—from the design of VOSS's unique glass bottle (inspired by the way fragrances are bottled in the perfume industry) to the bold premium pricing policy (at high-end restaurants where VOSS is served, it is not unusual for diners to receive, at the end of their meal, a water tab approaching three figures)—is instructive for the sheer calculation behind the brand's origins.

Incidentally, while VOSS considers itself a luxury brand, it is by no means alone in the ultra-premium bottled water sub-category. Packaged in a frosted glass bottle decorated with Swarovski crystals, Beverly Hills–based Bling H2O launched in 2006; at prices ranging from $20 to $40 for a 750-milliliter bottle, Bling has reportedly fetched $90 at some Las Vegas nightclubs. Other high-end brands include Canadian Can-Aqua, Tasmanian rainwater King Island Cloud Juice, Japanese Finé, Welsh Tau, and Icelandic Glacial.

For the full case study, which includes an overview of the

bottled water industry, see "VOSS Artesian Water of Norway," Harvard Business School Case Study 509-040.

The Heavenly Bed (page 68)

As I mention in "The Paradox of Progress," Westin Hotels (Starwood Hotels & Resorts) is credited with instigating what folks in the industry commonly refer to as the "hotel bed wars."* Prior to Westin's introduction of The Heavenly Bed, luxury hoteliers had always provided premium bedding to their guests, but what made Westin's initiative such a strong competitive salvo was that it was the industry's first branded offering, and the centerpiece of a multimillion-dollar marketing campaign. This raised the market stakes considerably, putting enormous pressure on competitors to copycat the move. Within a few years, virtually every major chain had committed to some kind of specialty bed.

Did The Heavenly Bed increase customer satisfaction among Westin Hotel guests? Well, according to Westin's internal market research, prior to the introduction of The Heavenly Bed, guests had given "comfort of bed" a ranking of 8.96 out of 10; after the introduction, that ranking increased to 9.19 out of 10. So if you believe the research, the $30 million investment moved the satisfaction score by roughly 2 percent. Meanwhile, given the difficulty in linking hotel market share to any single hotel attribute, such as bedding, it's hard to say whether The Heavenly Bed increased Westin's competitive position in the industry.

For the full case study, see "The Hotel Bed Wars," Harvard Business School Case Study 509-059.

---

*__Bed Wars.__ Definition: (Slang) The competition among hotel chains to attract customers by offering better and more elaborate bedding, including special mattresses, luxury sheets, and elaborate arrangements of pillows and bolsters. —From *The Travel Industry Dictionary*

Google (pages 109–113)

Google is one of those rare technology brands for which people have great affection despite its market dominance. Most hegemonic technology brands have difficulty retaining any kind of charm (think Microsoft), but Google has thus far escaped this fate. In fact, what I find most remarkable about Google is that many of its average users have absolutely no idea how Google makes money. Its interface is so intuitive, so simple, so stripped-down, that it feels almost noncommercial to use, despite the fact that it has become the most powerful advertising force in the industry. It is the rare category killer that manages to carry itself as an underdog. As *The Economist* describes it, Google is "the world's most valuable online advertising agency disguised as a search engine."

Here's how big Google has become: From being unprofitable in early 2000, Google was logging more than $6 billion in advertising revenue by 2005—more advertising than any single newspaper chain, magazine publisher, or television network sold that year. In 2008, Google brought in a whopping $21 billion in advertising revenue, and was still growing apace.

As Google has grown, its product portfolio has exploded. At launch, Google offered nothing more than its search engine. By 2009, this portfolio had expanded to include everything from email (Gmail) to photo editing (Picasa) to video (YouTube). Not surprisingly, this plethora of service offerings has created a tension with Google's commitment to its clean, uncluttered homepage aesthetic. It has even led to criticism—criticism with which I disagree, by the way—that Google is making a mistake in under-promoting its other products in order to protect the user experience. One industry observer described the issue this way: "The problem is that every time Google branches out, it struggles with the very thing that makes its search engine so successful: simplicity. . . . So Google can't showcase its plethora of new products without jeopardizing this sleek interface."

For the full case study, see "Google Advertising," Harvard Business School Case Study 507-038.

IKEA (pages 117–121)

IKEA is another one of those brands that manages to carry itself as an underdog even though it is anything but. The IKEA Group is in fact the world's top furniture retailer, and although it is privately held and does not release profit figures, its 2008 revenues topped 21 billion euros and its brand is considered to be among the most valuable in the world. Personally, I love the fact that a brand can be so completely forthright about what it asks of its customers and still come out a winner.

The IKEA website is a lesson in transparency. There's a section entitled "How to Shop at IKEA" that explicitly warns customers about the IKEA experience. It advises: "Be prepared. Make a list of anything you may need for your home. . . . Take measurements of spaces you want to fill with furniture. And be sure there's room in your car. You'll need it."

The site goes on to describe what customers can expect when they enter the store: "Everything you need to shop is available at the entrance: pencils, paper, tape measures, store guides, catalogs, shopping carts, shopping bags and strollers." It also notes that "picking up your purchases is an important part of IKEA's approach to customer involvement. Specifically, if you can do simple things like pick up your purchases and assemble them at home, we'll keep prices low."

A trip to IKEA requires what one cheeky reporter dubbed "IKEA stamina." According to this same reporter, without this endurance, shoppers become prone to "IKEA meltdown," symptoms of which include: extreme irritability, fatigue, and Svediphobia (fear of all things Swedish). It is this same "stamina" that apparently invigorates shoppers to be willing to assemble, for example, a multipiece storage unit once at home.

In homage to the almighty Allen wrench—a key instrument in IKEA's do-it-yourself business model—a sixteen-foot-tall version of the wrench stands outside of IKEA's world headquarters.

For the full case study, see "IKEA Invades America," Harvard Business School Case Study 504-094.

JetBlue (pages 111–112)

When JetBlue launched its inaugural flight out of JFK airport in early 2000, the brand's mission, according to then CEO David Neeleman, was to "bring humanity back to air travel." Pulling this off required a tricky balancing act. Delivering great service in this industry can be an expensive undertaking, so from the outset JetBlue broke with tradition by embracing relatively stringent cost-saving measures: The airline didn't serve free meals, it only offered coach seating, and it only flew out of less-trafficked airports. Yet JetBlue offset these cost-saving measures with honest-to-goodness frills: Every seat on the plane was spacious and leather-upholstered; all passengers were provided with their own video screen with satellite TV; biscotti, cookies, and blue tortilla chips were offered in flight. It's easy to take these kinds of benefits for granted today, but back in the early 2000s, these kinds of perks were unheard of in the discount end of the market.

Some have described JetBlue as "the lovechild of Southwest and Virgin Airlines," and the "Target of the skies," while others have used terms like "poverty chic" to describe JetBlue's unique blend of benefits. David Talbot, CEO of the online magazine *Salon,* has described the airline like this: JetBlue is "scrappy and independent, but seems like a premium travel experience at a discount price. I even like the fact that they don't have different classes. Everyone is in it together, like the Web ethic. It's democratic with a small 'd' and that's appealing."

Thirty years ago, Paul Theroux wrote, "You define a good flight by negatives . . . you didn't crash, you didn't throw up, you weren't late, you weren't nauseated by the food. And so you're grateful." To a large extent, this is still true today; when it comes to our attitudes toward air travel, we remain a hardened, cynical bunch. That's why I would argue that brands like JetBlue deserve a little credit for making a genuine attempt to offer a flying experience that is more than just tolerable, that dares to offer a few hints of pleasure along the way . . .

In-N-Out Burger (pages 121–122)

As I note in "Reversal," it's difficult to overstate how fanatical folks can be about In-N-Out Burger. In-N-Out's Facebook page has over 200,000 fans, and is a forum for devotees to share their tales of dedication: "I used to have to drive two hours to eat one and did it every two weeks," shares a typical fan. A forum on the page asks, "How far have you traveled for an In-N-Out Burger?" with respondents claiming to have driven hundreds of miles for a single meal.

In an industry in which competitors are constantly offering more variety, more options, more quickly, it takes a lot of company discipline to adhere so strictly to such an uncomplicated, unchanging value proposition. As a reporter once pointed out, when McDonald's announces, say, the addition of three new Premium Chicken sandwiches to its menu, what you're seeing is more menu expansion than In-N-Out has engaged in over its entire sixty-year history.

Even the toughest critics have only good things to say about In-N-Out. Eric Schlosser, author of a scathing review of the fast-food industry (*Fast Food Nation*), has gone on record as an admirer: "I think they're great," he has said. "It isn't health food, but it's food with integrity. It's the real deal." The reason for the praise? In-N-Out uses hand-leafed lettuce, potatoes peeled and cut on-site, shakes blended with real ice cream, and buns baked with slow-rising sponge dough. As for the beef, In-N-Out operates its own patty-making facility in California, where every chuck is individually examined. Of course, this commitment to non-processed, made-to-order, fresh food, combined with high demand, yields an average wait time of well over ten minutes, much longer than the industry standard. During peak times at newly opened locations, customers have been known to queue for up to two hours for a burger. But these customers understand that quality takes time, and so the delay becomes yet another rite in the religion that is In-N-Out.

An aside: Although I am the named author of a case study on this brand, I actually deserve very little credit for it. The heavy lifting was done by some students of mine (Lucy Cummings, Sonali Sampat, and Sam Thakarar), self-confessed In-N-Out freaks who were absolutely determined to capture the story of this brand on paper. See "In-N-Out Burger," Harvard Business School Case Study 503-096.

Sony AIBO (pages 129–137)

Although the Sony AIBO project described in "Breakaway" ultimately fell victim to Sony's cost-cutting initiatives, the case remains among my favorite to teach. As I tell my students, there are really only two reasons why a firm would ever bring a given product to market. The first is to take advantage of the product's revenue potential. This is what I refer to as "marketing to sell"—wherein the primary benchmark for the product's success is the product's actual sales results.

The second is what I refer to as "marketing to learn." The marketing mindset is markedly different here, because now the primary objective is to accumulate market learnings that can be incorporated into future iterations of the product—which means that at least in the short term the investment in the product cannot fairly be measured against the product's next-quarter P&L. I wrote the Sony AIBO case during an era in which Sony's dominance in the consumer technology domain was without rival, and the company was in a position to place long-term bets, support skunk works initiatives, and give its engineers lots of room to "play" with ideas. Alas, those days are long gone . . .

Still, the marketing experimentation you see in this case, along with the consumer response that this product generated, remains deeply revealing. The critical point in Sony's AIBO development process occurs when the managers explicitly begin asking themselves a set of core questions: What *is* this product? What could it *be*? After much creative deliberation, the team finally decides on a positioning strategy, a strategy that, as I noted earlier, ultimately becomes a transformative device: It transforms an instrumental product into a playful one; it transforms a series of product flaws ("the robot doesn't obey commands") into product benefits ("it's a pet with a mind of its own!"). I will never forget my interviews with dozens of AIBO owners, most of whom exhibited an almost astonishing degree of forgiveness with the product's many flaws, coupled with an equally astonishing degree of affection for their respective machines. As one of them told me, "Of course I know it's not alive—I'm not stupid. But it's so easy to forget that it's just a machine. The other day, I caught myself talking to it, you know, doggie-talk like 'C'mere you widdle puppy wuppy.' And I dunno, I couldn't help but feel . . . *psyched* when he responded, like hey, he *loves* me."

To me, this case demonstrates the extent to which the thoughtful framing of a product—specifically, the breakaway positioning of an otherwise flawed product—can create dramatic and extreme shifts in consumer behaviors, attitudes, and emotions.

For the full case study, see "Sony AIBO: The World's First Entertainment Robot," Harvard Business School Case Study 502-010.

Pull-Ups (pages 138–139)

When Kimberly-Clark introduced Huggies Pull-Ups Disposable Training Pants in 1989, the product was publicly targeted toward the "four million children who annually are ready to outgrow their need for diapers and begin toilet training." But the actual motivation behind the launch was to extend the life cycle of diaper-wearing toddlers, to keep them from dropping out of the diaper market even as they reached the ages of two, three, and four.

From the start, Pull-Ups were essentially diapers with an underwear-like form factor: They had elastic sides so that children could pull them up and down on their own, and a clothlike exterior sculpted to more closely resemble big-kid underwear, both in look and in feel. The tagline for Pull-Ups was "I'm a big kid now," and the promotional campaign was explicitly designed to create psychological separation from diapers (which were, of course, for babies).

The launch proved enormously successful for several reasons. First, not only were the firm's margins on Pull-Ups significantly higher (on a per-unit basis) than they were on the firm's traditional diaper products (due in part to the fact that competitive pressures tended to drive prices of the latter down), but the use of Pull-Ups greatly increased the number of total diapers worn in a child's life. As one retail analyst noted, Kimberly-Clark was able, in some instances, to triple the life cycle of its customers.

Second, Kimberly-Clark was able to reap the benefits of being the only real player in the training pants subcategory for close to a decade. In 1991, two years after the introduction of Pull-Ups, Kimberly-Clark was already ringing up sales approaching $500 million a year from the product line, leading *Brandweek* to observe: "It isn't often that the Procter & Gamble Co. of Cincinnati [Kimberly-Clark's primary competitor in this market] gets caught with its pants down. But that's exactly what seems to be happening in the emerging category of disposable training pants." In fact, it wasn't until 2002 that P&G was able to launch a viable competitive product (Easy Ups) in the market, and even today, P&G continues to play market share catch-up to Kimberly-Clark in this domain.

Cirque du Soleil (pages 140–141)

The production that thrust Cirque du Soleil into the entertainment spotlight was entitled, appropriately, *Le Cirque Réinventé*. The title was deliberately re-definitive. The idea was to re-create, to reinvent, to reconceptualize what a circus might be. Gone were the peanut shell–laden floors, the dusty air, the three-ring spectacle with the prancing animals. Indeed, tackiness of any sort was verboten. A *Washington Post* reviewer quipped, "If Barnum & Bailey is the Kmart of circuses, then this is the designer boutique."

Of course, becoming the "designer boutique" of circuses didn't happen overnight. René Dupéré, one of the original musical composers of Cirque du Soleil, has noted elsewhere that "people might think that we set out to reinvent the circus, and then just did it. But things don't happen that way. We were just a bunch of crazy people who wanted to do things, and little by little we came to a vision of what the modern circus could be."

Guy Laliberté, the founder of Cirque du Soleil, drew on a number of artistic sources for inspiration in developing the concept, and in fact the early shows made a huge impression for their seamless mélange of dance, theater, music, and gymnastics. The shows have "imagery as fantastical as that in a Fellini film and costumes as colorful and whimsical as anything that might show up on a Christian Lacroix runway," wrote the *Chicago Sun-Times*. It made sense that one of Cirque's most high-profile early performances occurred at the Los Angeles Arts Festival in 1987; the appearance was designed to feed the perception that circus performance could be a form of "high art, worthy of serious consideration."

Today, Cirque du Soleil performs on five continents and generates annual receipts in excess of $500 million. It has produced more than twenty shows since 1987, and it continues to garner international acclaim.

Swatch (pages 141–142)

Honestly, there aren't that many geniuses in business, but in my mind, Nicolas Hayek, the visionary behind the Swatch, could rightfully be labeled one. Given that it's been a couple of decades since the Swatch was introduced, it's easy to forget how radical the Swatch was in its initial incarnation. Before the Swatch came along, Swiss watches were a serious product; they were sold in the finest jewelry stores and in some cases were even treated as family heirlooms. By contrast, the Swatch was conceptualized as pure fashion accessory—frivolous, spontaneous, impulsive, and faddish—and the man who shepherded the Swatch idea from conception to introduction was Hayek.

Prior to launch, the company tested several Swatch prototypes in U.S. department stores to gauge how consumers would respond to the genre-busting product. The results were not encouraging. Still, Hayek decided to ignore the market research and proceed with the launch; he had already heard so many naysayers mock the idea of the Swatch that the lack of external validation no longer bothered him. As he put it at the time, "You can build mass-market products in countries like Switzerland or the United States only if you embrace the fantasy and imagination of your childhood and youth. . . . People may laugh—the CEO of a huge Swiss company talking about fantasy. [But] too many of Europe's large institutions—companies, governments, unions—are as rigid as prisons. They are all steel and cement and rules. We kill too many ideas by rejecting them without thinking about them, by laughing at them."

That said, there was an enormous amount of discipline behind the execution of Hayek's "fantasy." The company didn't necessarily have to reinvent the wheel here; instead, by borrowing heavily from the conventions of the fashion industry, it was able to present consumers with a number of psychological cues that reinforced Swatch's breakaway positioning. For example, the Swatch product line was managed unlike any other in the industry at the time: It changed on a seasonal basis; there were two collections a year; each collection was dramatically different from the one before; and there were no repeated production runs, which meant that collections were replaced before they could become outdated. In addition, there was tremendous product diversity: At any given time, a consumer could choose from a collection of at least seventy designs. This overwhelming number of models encouraged the perception that Swatches were accessories to be mixed-and-matched depending on one's outfit, mood, or taste. Again, although this kind of product strategy was unheard of in the watch industry, it was the norm in the world of fashion, where manufacturers were constantly struggling to stay ahead of fickle consumer tastes.

There is much to be learned from other components of the Swatch marketing strategy—the pricing strategy, the product design process, etc.—as well. For more details, see "The Birth of the Swatch," Harvard Business School Case Study 504-096.

Alessi (page 146)

Alessi is an Italian family-run business that has spent the last three decades reimagining what the ordinary household object might be. With Alessi, mundane utensils for the kitchen and table are transformed into chic, eye-catching pieces of art.

When the company began producing designer tea kettles and wine openers in the 1980s (designed by serious artists and architects such as Michael Graves and Alessandro Mendini), the world had never seen anything like them. And although today it has become commonplace for producers of household products to merge aesthetic design and function in striking ways—indeed, it is now possible to walk into a Target and experience the convergence of art and utility in just about every aisle—it is important to give credit where credit is due. Just as Swatch was responsible for giving birth to the watch-as-fashion-accessory trend that we now take for granted, Alessi was among the first players in the market to recognize the category-defying potential of something as inherently unsexy as a tea kettle.

For years, Alberto Alessi has been the creative force behind Alessi. Although he runs the business with his brothers and other family members, Alberto, the eldest grandson of the company founder, is the ultimate arbiter of the company's product line. Here is how he regards his responsibility: "I view my role as not unlike that of an art gallery director or a museum curator or a filmmaker. What I am trying to do is build a catalog, an eclectic catalog that contains lots of interesting contrasts."

I interviewed the Alessi brothers at length a few years ago. At one point, I asked Alberto if the company ever relied on market research to guide their product strategy. His response:

"No, in our case, it would be entirely inappropriate. To understand why, think about a car manufacturer. When a car manufacturer decides to produce a new car, what does it do? The thing it will do is conduct market research. It will ask consumers, "How do you envision the car of the future?" The poor consumer will respond by looking at existing cars and saying, "I like this part of the car, I don't like this part of the car." The car manufacturer will take this data, put it together, shake it up, and out comes a product briefing that is completely lacking in creativity. The end result is that all new cars look the same. This is how products end up being anonymous and boring.

At Alessi, I'm not really interested in what consumers think. I'm interested in cultivating the work of designers who will create transcendent designs. However, if I do my job well, I should be able to produce what consumers want, even before they know they want it.

For the full case study, see "Alessi: Evolution of an Italian Design Factory (A, B, C, D)," Harvard Business School Case Studies 504-018, 504-019, 504-020, 504-022.

MINI Cooper (pages 159–163)

The agency behind the launch of the MINI Cooper was Miami-based Crispin Porter + Bogusky, and as I mention in "Hostility," one of the riskier elements of the campaign was an explicit rejection of the idea that when it comes to automotive transport, size matters. Alex Bogusky, the executive creative director of the agency, told *Adweek* that, yes, "there were times we were nervous." But against all the market evidence indicating that Americans remained in love with their SUVs, the agency pushed hard for the counter-logical approach. In addition to the billboards that read "The SUV backlash begins here" were ones that proclaimed "Goliath lost," and "Soon, small will mean huge the way bad means good."

Sure enough, the campaign managed to attract consumers with a particular "MINI mindset." Internal market research indicated that MINI customers tended to be nonconformists, people who identified themselves as having creative hobbies and pursuits. One automotive analyst likened the brand's appeal as follows: "What do they say about Maine? Not many like it, but those that like it, love it." More broadly, the unorthodox campaign managed to boost consumer awareness of the brand from 2 percent to 60 percent in a single year.

Red Bull (pages 164–165)

Dietrich Mateschitz, the founder of Red Bull, has been known to say, "Red Bull isn't a drink, it's a way of life." Mateschitz understands that when it comes to easily commoditized products such as beverages, image is 90 percent of the game. This is why he has always encouraged the cultivation of the brand's mystique: "Without the old high school teacher telling his students Red Bull is evil—probably even a drug—it wouldn't seem as interesting."

As I note in "Hostility," what's instructive about Red Bull is the extent to which the brand's success can be attributed to the fact that its managers did all the things that a standard marketing textbook would say you should never do. Incidentally, I'm not the only one to notice this. Because Red Bull came out of nowhere to spawn a new subcategory in the beverage industry (it is possible to argue that the energy drink category wouldn't exist without Red Bull), much has been written about the brand and its unorthodox marketing approach. In his article "The Murketing of Red Bull," *New York Times* columnist Rob Walker writes, "Usually the wizards of branding want to be extremely clear about what their product is for and who's supposed to buy it. Red Bull does just the opposite. Everything about the company and its sole product is intentionally vague, even evasive. . . . You could argue that what Red Bull drinkers have in common is a taste for the edgy and faintly dangerous. But what does this really mean? Obviously any attempt to articulate such a thing would immediately destroy it."

Later in the article, Walker interviews some college students about Red Bull, including Kaytie Pickett, a dormitory resident assistant at Tulane University. "It's really a kind of fashionable drink," she says to Walker. "You see the fashionable sorority girls buying their can of Red Bull with their Marlboro Lights. It's like: 'Look, I can afford to pay $3 for this ridiculous drink.'"

Birkenstock (page 166)

There are few brands that can claim the kind of stark, un-yielding, and clearly defined set of connotations that the word "Birkenstock" brings to mind. With its unaestheticized, prac-tical sandals, clogs, and shoes, Birkenstock is a stubborn bo-hemian that prides itself on its granola-crunching, anti-chic ethos. The brand website puts it this way:

> Cork. Leather. A buckle or two. A simple idea that's made feet happy for over two hundred years. Made in Germany since 1774 (with a few minor design tweaks in the meantime). No smoke. No mirrors. No gizmos. You walk, the shoe molds to your foot. You feel good. We feel good. That's the deal.

The brand made its way to America on the feet of Margot Fraser, who stumbled upon the sandals while vacationing in Germany in the 1960s. When she began importing the shoes to the States, general shoe retailers scoffed at the "hideous" and "homely" things. As a result, one of the first places where Birkenstocks were sold was in health food stores in Berkeley.

Today, of course, Birkenstocks can be found just about any-where, and although the company has experimented through-out the years with various design partnerships (with, for example, the renowned architect Yves Behar and supermodel Heidi Klum), it has never strayed from its commitment to its bestselling classics: the Arizona and the Boston Clog, neither of which will ever win a beauty contest. Manolo the Shoe-Blogger (the "king of the fashion blogosphere," says *UK Vogue*), bemoans the brand in his Gallery of Horrors:

> Perhaps the ugliest, most unstylish shoe ever manufac-tured. This shoe, it looks like it was put together by blind medieval monks, for wear by the peasants of the mud.

Marmite (pages 164–165)

Depending on who you ask, Marmite is either "the closest thing to eating old motor oil" or "the nectar of the gods." Oliver Bradley, a spokesperson for the brand, has gone on record saying, "[We] know that for 100 years, a whole lot of people have hated it. . . . [O]ur brand, unlike others, has the confidence and cheekiness to say 'we know that and we don't care.'" Indeed, the slogan "You either love it or hate it" has headlined the brand's advertising campaigns for the past thirteen years.

Marmite has been around for more than a century, and for many Brits, eating Marmite on buttered toast is their earliest culinary memory. In World War II, Marmite was a staple for British troops, although even back in those days, its parent company acknowledged that "soldiers were as likely to spread Marmite under the zipper area of their pants to stave off infection as they were to eat it."

As with most things, the best place to get a sense of the brand without actually having to sample it yourself is online. Here, the degree of polarization is extreme even by hostile brand standards. There are more than 200,000 fans claiming their love for the goo on Marmite's Facebook page; at the same time, there are hundreds of groups avowing complete disgust with the stuff. Sample comments include: "I'd rather remove my own spleen with a rusty fork and feed it to a penguin dressed in a clown outfit than eat [Marmite]"; "one of the most vile creations man has ever made"; and "Marmite is made from ear wax, fox droppings and the tears of a tramp."

It is estimated that Brits take more than 8 million jars of Marmite with them on vacation, and that the staple can be found in one in every four kitchens in England.

A Bathing Ape (pages 168–169)

The founder of A Bathing Ape is "Nigo" (real name: Tomoaki Nagao), a Japanese music producer and DJ whose nickname literally means "number two" in Japanese. Nigo is both famously and idiosyncratically abstruse, despite having become, according to some reports, the wealthiest fashion designer in his country.

Although BAPE is clearly a Japanese brand, it has managed to penetrate the American underground zeitgeist, at least indirectly, through its adoption by popular entertainers in this country. Pharrell Williams, Jay Z, Lil Wayne, and Young Jeezy are some of the hip-hop personalities known to wear the brand. That said, BAPE products remain pretty tough to get one's hands on here in the United States. If you do decide to go hunting for them, a word of caution: There are lots of counterfeit BAPEs out there (the street term for these counterfeits is "FAPEs"), no doubt a result of the relative inaccessibility of authentic BAPEs, not to mention their hefty price tags.

Hollister (pages 171–172)

Hollister is the younger, less-expensive sibling brand of Abercrombie & Fitch. Its target demographic appears to be high schoolers (although many middle schoolers shop there, too), but its actual target market is narrower than that: Hollister chases popular, thin, beautiful kids. Here is Mike Jeffries, the CEO of Abercrombie, speaking to *Salon*:

> Candidly, we go after the cool kids. We go after the attractive all-American kid with a great attitude and a lot of friends. A lot of people don't belong [in our clothes], and they can't belong. Are we exclusionary? Absolutely. Those companies that are in trouble are trying to target everybody: young, old, fat, skinny. But then you become totally vanilla. You don't alienate anybody, but you don't excite anybody, either.

Given this, everything about the Hollister in-store experience is designed to dichotomize, to galvanize enemies and devotees with equal force. It begins on the approach. The store itself is hidden, sequestered behind a faux-California beach bungalow facade, which means that window-shopping is impossible. Inside the store, the lighting is dim, the ceilings are low, and the music (a punk-emo-indie-pop mix) is deafening. In fact, the tunes are so loud that an Arizona newspaper did an undercover report on the in-store decibel levels—the noise registered at ninety, which is the maximum permissible level for an employee to be forced to endure for eight hours. Understandably, most parents hate the place.

Hollister's in-store employees are called "models," and the females in particular are all young, thin, and pretty. The firm has been hit with lawsuits alleging that the brand discriminates against minorities in its hiring practices and forces employees to adopt improper dress codes. (Both suits were eventually settled, but not without significant publicity.) The brand advertising is highly sexualized, and the sizing of the brand is deliberately intended to keep the non-thin crowd away.

For all of this effort, what is there to show? As of 2009, more than five hundred stores, and $1.5 billion in annual sales.

Benetton (pages 175–177)

The Benetton website contains a rather stunning historical archive of samples from its advertising campaigns throughout the years. All of the more controversial images are there, along with an explanation of the firm's advertising and brand philosophy.

As a conceptual exercise, I have found teaching this case to be immensely valuable, because it forces students to think not only about what advertising is, but perhaps more important about what advertising could or even should be. When I run the Benetton discussion, I will often flash quotes from various industry observers on a screen at the front of the class:

Advertising should sell happiness. . . . This pair [Toscani and Benetton] have understood that society is adrift, and they have chosen the easy path: instead of extending a lifebuoy, they are pushing society's head down further underwater, rubbing its nose in sex, in AIDS, in shit. (Jacques Séguéla, EuroRSCG)

[Benetton's] "advertising" is totally irrelevant to the products he is meant to be selling. . . . You can put a four-letter word in a headline and it will certainly be noticed, but it doesn't mean I like you for it. (Ced Vidler, Lintas Worldwide)

Benetton has restated a truth about successful advertising . . . that to create a distinctive "culture" around a brand is . . . often more important than a practical selling benefit. (James Lowther, Saatchi & Saatchi)

I will also highlight responses to this criticism from Benetton and Toscani:

Advertisers have done a lot of social damage . . . using fake images and fake dreams to sell us their products, so that today if you are a girl you really are a nobody if you don't look like Isabella Rossellini . . .

Advertising is the richest and most powerful form of communication in the world. . . . Ad agencies are obsolete. . . . They create a false reality and want people to believe in it. We show reality and we're criticised for it.

I haven't written my own case study on this brand because several excellent case studies already exist, including one out of INSEAD (written by Christian Pinson and Vikas Tibrewala) that includes the quotes highlighted above.

Apple (pages 186–188)

So much has been written about Apple that it feels superfluous to add anything here. Let me just say that out of the hundreds of articles that have attempted to capture Apple's iconoclasm throughout the years, the one with the best headline is a *Wired* magazine piece from 2008 entitled "How Apple Got Everything Right by Doing Everything Wrong." That headline just about nails it, in my view. The sidebar to the article goes on to outline five core Silicon Valley principles that Apple defies as a matter of course. Here are two examples of Apple rule breaking, excerpted from this article:

Silicon Valley Rule: COMMUNICATE. Tell your fans what you're up to so they feel a connection to your company. Hiring difficulties? New strategies? Digestive problems? Blog 'em! Customers will feel more invested and more loyal. Plus, their comments could give you some good ideas.

Apple Rule: Never talk to the press. Shut down rumor blogs. Threaten to sue children who send you their ideas. Never leak product news until you're ready to announce it. Then use that discipline to create buzz and win coverage with every announcement.

Silicon Valley Rule: LOVE YOUR CUSTOMERS. Make sure to lavish affection on your clients, and try to ensure that every one of them has a positive experience. Anyone can post a withering review on Yelp or Amazon, so you can't afford to let a single complaint go unaddressed.

Apple Rule: Please yourself, not your fans. Release iMacs without floppy drives. Release MacBook Airs without optical drives. Cut the price of an iPhone by

$200 two months after its introduction; when early adopters complain, offer them a $100 gift certificate.

Harley-Davidson (pages 188–191)

In the 1950s and 1960s, biker clubs were populated by leather-and-jean-clad rebels committed to the outlaw lifestyle. Hunter S. Thompson described the culture of the most notorious biker club of the era in his book *Hell's Angels: A Strange and Terrible Saga of the Outlaw Motorcycle Gangs* (1966). What held these clubs together was a shared code of rebellion and, as Thompson puts it, "a mindless kind of loyalty." Routes were organized by the bikers themselves, determined largely by the desire to avoid getting stuck by "tight speed limits, lack of signs, [or] unusual laws." Along the way, there were the inevitable skirmishes with police, arrests, and fights with other biker clubs; meanwhile, the outlaw bike of choice happened to be a Harley.

Today, the largest biker club in the world is no longer an organic creation; rather, it is run by Harley itself. The first year of membership in H.O.G. (the Harley Owners Group) is free with the purchase of a Harley, and among the benefits of membership are access to company-organized gatherings and rallies, as well as access to a members-only website. A recent Harley-organized celebration began with 105 starting points across the country, which then converged to 25 different routes, all ending in Milwaukee. The last time Harley held its own anniversary rally in its hometown, it had no trouble selling out the allotted 125,000 slots. For bikers who want to organize their own cross-country rides, Harley provides (via its website and its membership manual) road guides, trip planners, and useful tips and pointers. Even at biker rallies not officially sponsored by Harley (e.g., Sturgis and Daytona), the Milwaukee brand has an overwhelming presence; according to estimates, roughly 90 percent of the bikes at Daytona carry the Harley brand.

In short, Harley does just about everything it can to cultivate the riders' sense of belonging, to provide a platform for fraternizing and bonding, and to support the mythology of the biker lifestyle.

Dove Real Beauty (pages 191–194)

My colleague John Deighton has written a compelling case study about the Dove Campaign for Real Beauty. According to his research, the development of the controversial campaign created a good deal of internal angst within the company. One of the managers associated with the campaign characterized the concerns this way: "When you talk of real beauty, do you lose the aspirational element? Are consumers going to be inspired to buy a brand that doesn't promise to take you to a new level of attractiveness? Debunking the beauty myth brings with it the danger that you are debunking the whole reason to spend a little more money for the product. You're setting yourself up to be an ordinary brand."

Sure enough, the launch of the campaign met with some shrill criticism. Richard Roeper, a *Chicago Sun-Times* editorialist, revealed his brutish side in offering this comment: "Chunky women in their underwear have surrounded my house. . . . I find these ads a little unsettling. If I want to see plump gals baring too much skin, I'll go to Taste of Chicago, OK?" (I know, what a classy guy . . .) Even today, the public debate over the campaign continues on blogs, chat forums, YouTube, and the like.

Meanwhile, Dove has experienced a period of healthy growth and brand rejuvenation. Personally, I love brands that aren't afraid to initiate or engage us in topical dialogue.

For the full case study, see John Deighton, "Dove: Evolution of a Brand," Harvard Business School Case Study 508-047.

acknowledgments

For his assistance in bringing this book to market, I would like to thank my literary agent, Rafe Sagalyn. Rafe has been my guide to the world of book publishing. He is experienced and thoughtful, straightforward and unafraid. He was the first person, other than my husband and my best friend, that I showed this manuscript to, and he immediately understood what I was trying to do. Since then, he has been my advocate and adviser, and for that I am immensely grateful.

My editor at Crown was John Mahaney. John not only put considerable energy and care into this book, but he gave patient consideration to every little concern that I voiced along the way. John is a true veteran, and as a rookie author, I felt fortunate to be guided by his steady hand. Lynn Carruthers developed all of the sketches for the book. Lynn is a gifted artist, and I like to believe that there was a serendipity about the way our paths crossed such that I was able to coax her into this project. Jenna Bernhardson was my research assistant for this book. What I appreciate about Jenna is that despite possessing all of the productive characteristics of a classic Type A (an obsessive attention to detail, a relentless work ethic), she is one of the most laid-back, easygoing people you will ever meet. Jenna came to work for me straight out of college and all I can say is, the sky is the limit for this talented young woman. Scott Moore has been my administrative assistant for the past seven years, and (there is really no other way to put this) he is simply the best. He also happens to be the most fastidious dresser I have ever met, and although it used to feel strange to have an assistant who spends more on clothes than I do, I've long since gotten over it.

A very special thank-you goes to my students, without whom this book would surely not exist. Most of the ideas presented in this book were offered to them first, because I knew that they would push back, they would force refinement. Throughout the years, they have made the classroom a wonderful laboratory for exploration for me, and I am deeply indebted to them.

Although the following people were not directly involved in the development of this book, I would like to thank them for their general counsel throughout the years. David Bell and John Deighton are colleagues of mine at the Harvard Business School; they believed in and encouraged my research long before the others. I would also like to thank my colleague Frances Frei, who has had my back since day one. The most succinct way for me to describe Frances to you is to say that she is someone who, no matter the context, no matter the delicacies of the situation, always speaks truth to power, sensitivities be damned, and when you see that kind of forthrightness coming from a woman operating in an otherwise restrained environment, it is a righteous thing, I tell you, a rare sight to behold.

On a more personal note, I have three sisters, Rachel, Hannah, and Sunita. In terms of the distribution of family characteristics, I can tell you that Rachel got the family sanity, Hannah got the sweetness, and Sunita has (thankfully) brought us all a little style. We are as different as siblings can be, but because the ethos of sisterhood runs strong in our family, they have been with me through every turn. I am grateful to all three of them for their steady kinship and support.

I would like to offer a few extended words for my closest friend, Gail. I know that female friendship can be an extraordinary thing at any age, but what I have found in the course of my friendship with Gail is that it can be particularly extraordinary in the middle years. These are the tumultuous years, after all, the years of child rearing and career building, the years during which it all seems to come together at once: the accomplishments and the defeats, the separations and the loss. In the near decade in which we have known each other, Gail and I have supported each other through every up and down. Meanwhile, as our husbands will tell you, we always seem to find ourselves neck-deep in some mischief, too, which is one of the reasons I consider her so much more than a friend—she is an accomplice, a co-conspirator if you will, of the very best kind. Along with my husband, Gail read every word of every draft of this book, and offered not only reinforcement along the way, but more important, reassurance that the words were not too trivial or too personal to merit an audience larger than the two of them.

Finally, I would like to thank my husband and children, to whom this book is dedicated. To paint you a picture: My older son, Jalen, is one of those kinds of kids who has a maturity about him that belies his chronological age, such that if you were to meet him and look at him, I mean *really* look at him, what you would see is a wise and benevolent man biding his time in the body of a child. My younger son, Tailo, on the other hand, is all lightning and free spirit; he is, and will always be, my irrepressible Peter Pan. These two boys have influenced the way that I look at the world in ways that only a mother can understand. Their warmth, their presence, their intelligence, and their joy are here, in this book, on every page, in every sentence. To this day, every little thing about them infuses my thoughts, my work, my writing, and my teaching, and although I'd be hard-pressed to explain exactly why, I know that I am a clearer thinker for it.

As for my husband, all I will say here is this. What I find most precious about the relationship we have together is that

it is uncomplicated. There is laughter, there is listening, there
is loyalty, there is love. When you have this kind of simplicity
in your life, I have discovered, it centers you. This is what
Robert does for me; he centers me. Truth be told, I initially
found the prospect of writing a book to be an unnerving
thing. But what gave me the confidence to begin putting
words to paper was knowing that he would be my first
reader . . . *it's just my voice to his ears,* I kept telling myself.
And it was this internal correspondence with him that made
it possible for me to begin. This is a man who, on the day he
met my father, made many promises, and has kept every one.
To the extent that the voice in here rings authentic, I hope he
knows that the secret credit belongs to him.

acknowledgments

index

about the author

Youngme Moon is the Donald K. David Professor at the Harvard Business School, where she teaches one of the most popular courses in the school's curriculum. She has received a number of awards for teaching excellence, and has published some of the bestselling business case studies in the world. She holds degrees from Yale University and Stanford University, and lives in Brookline, Massachusetts, with her husband and two sons.